LANCASTER AT WORK

BUSINESS IN LANCASTER COUNTY, PENNSYLVANIA

Lancaster County Historical Society

Acknowledgments

The Lancaster County Historical Society extends its thanks to Michael L. Abel, FLCHS, for his time and devotion to producing this volume; Pamela E. Hall, William E. Krantz, and James F. Ward for their assistance; the many local businesses that donated photographs to our collections; and volunteers Patricia B. Keene, Ph.D., and J. Roger Stemen for their years of dedication to the Photograph Collection.

Front cover: F. C. Gerlitzki painting a house. See page 17 for details. LCHS 2-03-08-26
Previous page: Customers shop at J. C. Leaman's grocery store on a busy day in 1915. The Leaman family ran the grocery store in the 100 block of South Queen Street until the 1930s. LCHS D-11-04-11
Back cover (clockwise from top right): Typing at Union Saving Systems, D-12-04-17; giving a polio shot at Lancaster General Hospital, A-08-01-86; organizing at the Welfare Federation, D-04-01-47; waiting for customers at Tshudy's Oyster Bar & Saloon, A-09-02-28; making concrete tiles at Lancaster Concrete Tile Company, D-11-03-46; shelling pecans at Keystone Pecan Company, D-11-02-92; selling watches in John Sensenig's jewelry store, D-12-02-65.

Project Manager: Marianne Heckles
Editors: James T. Alton; Thomas R. Ryan, Ph.D.
Design: Michael L. Abel, FLCHS
Printed by Cadmus Communications, Ephrata, Pennsylvania

ISBN-10: 0-9740162-3-3
ISBN-13: 978-0-9740162-3-8
Library of Congress Control Number: 2006935843

Published by Lancaster County Historical Society
230 North President Avenue, Lancaster, Pennsylvania 17603
www.lancasterhistory.org

Contents

The Lancaster County Historical Society thanks the following businesses for their generous support of this book.

Presenting Sponsor

Supporting Sponsors

Contributing Sponsors

Dutch Gold Honey • Wilco Electric, Inc. • Goodville Mutual Casualty Company

Foreword

The time we spend at work, or in some sort of productive labor, accounts for at least one third of most of our days on earth. Whether we work unpaid in the home or out in the larger work force of paid laborers, salaried employees, independent entrepreneurs, or professionals of one sort or another, work often defines who we are. Of course we *are* more than what we *do*. Nonetheless, in our capitalist society, how we choose to earn our living is often central to how we understand ourselves and how others perceive us.

Yet for all of the time we spend working, it seems that we often take the experience for granted. We forget to assemble the bits and pieces of the past that help us, and others, remember our lives at work. Fortunately some of our forebears, over the years and across the centuries, took a moment here and there to record Lancastrians at work using the camera.

Photographs have an immediacy that puts us directly in touch with the past. Unlike diaries, letters, or other written records, photos bring us visually into familiar yet foreign spaces and place us inside the long-gone historical moment. We ponder a single photo for hours searching for clues and hints, opening our senses to multiple layers of meaning. Through the magic of chemicals, paper, and light, photographs draw us into their black-and-white world and temporarily steal us away.

With this second volume in our series of images from the collections of the Lancaster County Historical Society, we offer you a glimpse of work and industry in Lancaster County over the years. These images represent the best of the more than 15,000 photographs preserved for all time in our collections. The entire collection is available for your viewing pleasure with the click of a mouse at our headquarters on the corner of Marietta and North President Avenues. We will be glad to make high-quality reproductions of any of our images for your personal enjoyment.

Like our other collections, the Photograph Collection continues to grow through new acquisitions, gifts, and an occasional purchase. Maybe you have old photos of Lancaster people and places that you would like to see preserved for future generations. With a strong commitment to chronicling the history of twentieth-century Lancaster County we are very interested in adding such images to our collection. That is why we are here—to chronicle the history of our communities, to preserve the memories of people who have called Lancaster County their home, and to make these precious pieces of the past easily accessible for everyone to learn from and enjoy. If you would like to donate a photo, please call us at 717-392-4633, and let us know.

Thank you for continuing this photographic journey with us into Lancaster's past. I trust you will enjoy not only the photos but also the thoughtful introduction by nonagenarian (and Fellow of the Lancaster County Historical Society) Gerry Lestz, as well as the illuminating chapter introductions by members of our Publications Committee and an area scholar. Stay tuned for future volumes in this series. Who knows—you just might find someone you know staring at you from the past!

Thomas R. Ryan, Ph.D.
Executive Director
Lancaster County Historical Society

Introduction

Gerald S. Lestz

Dawn to dusk set the hours for the earliest work patterns in Lancaster County. The first settlers, in 1710, had to start from scratch to build their own barns and homes and till some of the most fertile acres on the face of the globe. Work came first; there was little time to relax. That work ethic, which is now firmly set in any description of Lancaster County, was thus displayed early in the eighteenth century. It remains fully evident after nearly 300 years among the descendants of the earliest families and the thousands who have moved in from innumerable places of origin.

Isaac S. "Ike" Tshudy, right, delivers oil to a family near Bowmansville, circa 1930. Tshudy worked for Eli S. Good's Gulf service station, which was located behind the Bowmansville Hotel in Bowmansville. Eli's widow, Annie, ran the business for a short time after his death.
LCHS 2-10-02-67

Out of those pioneer beginnings has emerged a tremendous array of energy that drives a major economic force. Lancaster County today is blazingly alive with all kinds of enterprises—from those of resourceful individuals who make furniture, paint portraits, bake cakes, and sell plants, to the big organizations that manage hospitals, operate colleges and universities, and manufacture flooring, computer software, and tractors. With one of the healthiest economies in the nation, Lancaster County does business in the billions of dollars, provides services to millions of tourists, and stays in the forefront of developments in industry, commerce, science, and culture.

What goes on today has evolved from what went on from the beginning. The present and past are inextricably intertwined.

PIONEERING AND THE WORK ETHIC

Farming was the primary occupation of the first settlers, around what is known as the Hans Herr House in West Lampeter Township. The sturdy surviving stone home with the date 1719 carved

A Turkey Hill Dairy milkman makes a home delivery in 1963. To get his customers fresh milk before breakfast, he started at the plant around 3 a.m., loaded his truck, spread crushed ice over the cases of milk, and covered them with heavy blankets to keep them cool.
LCHS 2-10-03-81

into its lintel is one of the oldest homes in the county, a Mennonite landmark. It served also as an early meetinghouse.

The soil was superb, but hard work in husbandry brought the early recognition. Lancaster grain won national status. Farmers were praised when people began to call Lancaster County "the Garden Spot"—whether it be of Pennsylvania or of all America.

To be able to plant and till, the first settlers had to tame "Penn's Woods" and cut down tremendous amounts of timber. They followed the black walnut, recognizing that black walnuts thrived where the land was most fertile. But when any trees had to be removed to make way for plowing, they were cut—by hand with primitive tools.

After Lancaster was established as the county seat in 1730, proprietor Andrew Hamilton set aside land on his map for a market place. As the hamlet grew a permanent farm-town relationship became established. The farm market became the hub of commerce and was elemental to social life. When an Indian treaty meeting was held in the Center Square in 1744, a young man who came here as a clerk was able to buy foodstuffs near his lodgings. William Marshe, the secretary to the Maryland commissioners forming the Treaty of Lancaster, wrote in his diary on June 21, 1744, "They have a very good market in this town. Well filled with provisions of all kinds and prodigiously cheap." He was not complimentary of other aspects of Lancaster, but his were the first words of praise for the market.

"Standing on market" was what the farmers did, and going to market was what the townspeople did. They found all manner of fresh fruits and vegetables, dressed poultry and game, and other choice comestibles. The interchange was very satisfying. Residents had their favorite vendors; they gave each other news of births, deaths, weddings, and much else. When the Revolutionary War began and numerous Philadelphians moved to Lancaster to evade the British, their numbers included Christopher Marshall, an apothecary who became a noted diarist. He wrote of hearing war news when he attended market.

The earliest craftsmen had skills in carpentry, construction, forging of tools, blacksmithing in general, building wagons, and making guns. Whereas farmers gathered stones from the fields to build barns and houses and had some ability to make what they needed, those who specialized in artisanship found customers among them.

Conestoga wagons, those huge lumbering "ships of commerce," were all made by hand. Even though uniform in appearance to the untrained eye, they showed individual handiwork. Wood and iron were basic; the canopies were hand-woven. They roamed the roads by the thousands, first linking the commerce within the county, and then beyond. Their makers and operators were intrinsic to the growth of the American business of carrying freight—and passengers.

Rifles, first made near Willow Street in a shop still marked as the place of origin, were also fabricated by hand, each an individual piece. During the Revolutionary War the British feared them as "widow-makers." As Daniel Boone and other Pennsylvanians moved out with their rifles, the guns became known as "Pennsylvania rifles" and then as "Kentucky rifles." They were among the American weapons fired in vain at the Alamo.

While farm and transportation needs were being met, craftsmen emerged in other fields. They catered to those leaving the county, or passing through, to make the trek to the western and southern frontiers. As Lancaster became the jumping-off place for these pioneers, the number of suppliers for the journey increased.

Silversmiths became prominent members of the small community, beginning a few years after the town's establishment. Evidently many of the silver items made were for the Indian trade, to be exchanged with tribesmen for furs. Joseph Simon, who built up extensive lines of commerce with the Indians extending into Ohio, was the major customer for these pieces, which were coined in the thousands. Silver pieces were also made for use of residents' households; some of these pieces are extant today. Jewelry shops, a natural outgrowth of the craftsmen's quarters, became a fixed part of the local business world.

Furniture making evolved as new generations of prospering families sought to brighten their homes. Many pieces sold today as choice antiques were made in Lancaster, including tall case clocks (later called grandfather clocks), settees, side chairs, arm chairs, and all the usual furniture forms. Often the furniture maker or seller also advertised wood coffins, some of them custom-made. In Strasburg, the Bachman Funeral Home is owned today by eighth-generation family

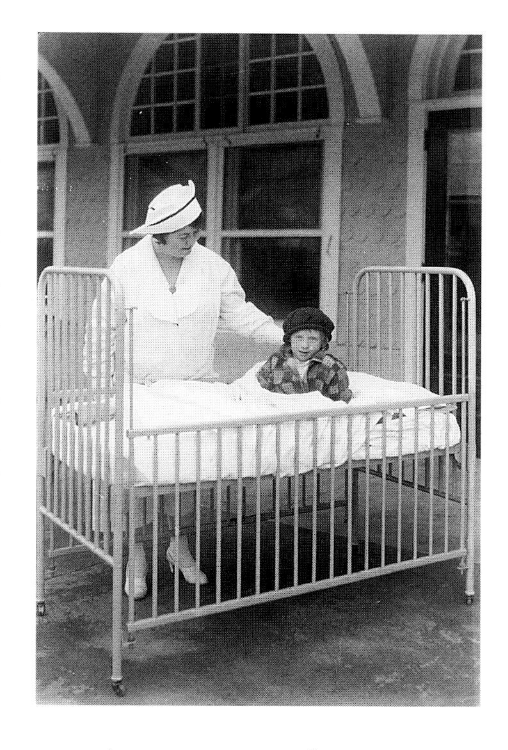

A nurse ensures that a young tuberculosis patient gets lots of fresh air at Rossmere Sanitarium, circa 1925, the year the facility opened to provide medical care to TB patients. Located at 600 Juliette Avenue, it closed its doors in 1957. LCHS D-02-02-37

Kenneth C. Myers, the late owner of Kegel's Produce in Lancaster, sorts tomatoes, 1961. The company, now located on Old Tree Drive, started in downtown Lancaster in the early 1930s as a fruit stand outside the Lancaster County Courthouse.
LCHS 2-10-03-44

members, dating back to coffin- and furniture-maker Johannes.

With the proliferation of grain from local farms, it was a natural connection for local brewmasters to start making beer in quantity. Distilleries for making whiskey had been plentiful here (making Lancaster County a leader in that form of endeavor), but as the nineteenth century moved along the number of breweries grew exponentially. Breweries ranked among the largest industrial buildings; mechanization aided in the bottling and labeling of the foamy products.

Hotels and taverns grew in number to meet rising demand. Completion of the Philadelphia–Lancaster Turnpike in 1791, the first macadamized road in the nation, brought with it the claim that there was a tavern for every mile. Accommodations "for man and beast" were not always the best, and guests frequently had to sleep five to a bed or on the floor, but business was brisk. In the city the array of brightly painted hostelry signs provided a streetside art gallery.

While there is full continuation and expansion of the brainpower and energy to conduct business, the kinds of businesses and job descriptions have changed over the years. Some titles go on, such as doctor, lawyer, teacher, candy maker, and merchant, but a look back shows how times and jobs have changed.

In 1860 the county had manufacturers of horse-drawn farm equipment and horse-drawn carriages, barrel-makers, cotton coverlet manufacturers, firearms makers, auger makers, makers of steel for railroads, liquor distillers, nickel mine operators, saddle makers, ship and boat builders, umbrella and parasol makers, and wool carders. Workers toiled on ferry boats and ferries, kept road toll booths, drove stage coaches, distilled coal oil, entertained as jugglers, ran livery stables, peddled the highways in horse-drawn carts or on foot, kept city street lights burning, served as scriveners to write letters for the illiterate, hand-rolled cigars, and rang church bells by hand.

As times changed, people adapted.

WORKING WOMEN

For women, the ancient adage, "A woman's place is in the home," guided much of Lancaster County life from the early 1700s into the World War I-era of the 1920s. The first farm women cooked, sewed, produced children, served as the family doctor, baked, gathered fruits and crops, and often helped in the heavier work of the farm. They were tied to home and family come what may. Yet some women broke through barriers and won honor for what they did, even as far back as Colonial times.

Women initially worked outside the home mainly as teachers or office aides. They were given the opportunity to work in a factory when the Conestoga Cotton Mills opened on South Prince Street about 1845. Most of the jobs involved tending machines. Later, as small shops evolved into larger stores, women found jobs as clerks.

An employee of the Keystone Pecan Company packs up cans of Pecano pecan meal to be shipped to customers throughout the country in 1927. LCHS D-11-02-89

In modern times, "Rosie the Riveter" became the national role model for women who took jobs in defense work to aid the military. Some of the work they handled had formerly been considered the preserve of men. After World War II, the gates opened further for women. Some encountered a "glass ceiling" in terms of pay and responsibilities, but the numbers of working women in Lancaster County have increased steadily.

OUTSTANDING INDIVIDUALS

Hard work involves both the mind and the body. Physical labor in itself is not the sole factor in the success of an innovator or a producer. The brain must be involved for best results. Ingenuity, ambition, initiative, and energetic action all factor into the careers of outstanding persons. Often, the ability to see a need that others have not recognized is what makes the difference between reaching the top and failing. Sustained tenaciousness and self-guided insistence on integrity are essential to making one's mark.

Over the centuries, thousands of men and women have won distinction for their achievements in making Lancaster County what it is today. Only a partial listing can be offered here, as representative of untold others.

John K. Galebach smoothes a floor with a power sander in a photograph taken in 1952 for *Country Gentleman* magazine. He founded Galebach's Floor Finishing after the invention of the power sander.
LCHS 2-10-02-84

Susannah Wright in Columbia took benevolent care of the ill, corresponded with Benjamin Franklin and others, and spun such fine silk out of worm-begotten fibers that she could make the gift of a length of fabric to the queen in London. Born in the late 1600s, she became an all-time role model.

William Henry Stiegel was a pre-Industrial Revolution industrialist who arrived in this country in 1750 to seek a new life. He became renowned as a manufacturer of glass in days when that enterprise was new. He lived in baronial style and produced glass that is to this day treasured for its beauty and quality.

Madame Ferree, who buttonholed William Penn in London for aid, led a settlement of fellow French Huguenots to build homes near what is now Paradise. She was befriended by a considerate Indian chief, Tanawa, who apparently admired her grit.

Madame LeTort, in Manor Township, ran the farm when her husband was off trapping or trading. She spied on Indians who showed too much interest in her crops.

Christopher Heyne, like Stiegel an immigrant from Germany, sold hardware but also developed a skill with metals. His pewter, especially in vessels made for churches, became renowned, and even though he was not identified as the maker until the twentieth century, his works are treasured today.

Christopher Demuth married into a family of tobacconists and founded a tobacco shop in 1770, which is nationally recognized as the oldest in America. He was followed in ownership by generations of family members, who operated the business well into the twentieth century. The store remains open today.

Edward Hand came to this country as a physician and a British military officer. He transformed into an early advocate of severing ties with Britain. Rising to become George Washington's adjutant general, Hand was elected mayor and served as a local spokesman in the drive to have Lancaster named the nation's capital.

George Ross was an attorney who brought Benjamin West to Lancaster to paint family portraits, which are extant today. Ross became a member of the Continental Congress and a signer of the Declaration of Independence.

The Reverend Henry Ernst Muhlenberg was a master of botany who became known as "the

American Linnaeus," high praise indeed considering that his primary profession was serving as pastor of Trinity Lutheran Church. He so enjoyed walking—to study plants in their native habitats or to attend meetings of the American Philosophical Society in Philadelphia—that he was dubbed "the Great Pedestrian."

Robert Fulton was an artist and an engineer with numerous patents. He invented a torpedo for underseas warfare, as well as a submarine, trying in vain to gain backing from Napoleon in France, and the British. His first steamboat, called by critics "Fulton's Folly," ushered in an era of technological progress unprecedented in American history.

James Buchanan, born near Mercersburg, developed as a Lancaster barrister and politico, gaining votes despite being thwarted by William Coleman, the millionaire father of the young woman he hoped to marry. Her early death haunted the later "Bachelor President." Unable to prevent the Civil War, he suffered the consequences engulfed in controversy.

Thaddeus Stevens, also an attorney, overcame the effects of a "club foot," which made him lame and was looked upon by his detractors as a tribulation from the devil. He tried unsuccessfully to unseat President Andrew Johnson. Stevens is best known today as a friend of enslaved African-Americans and the father of legislation that advanced civil rights and public education.

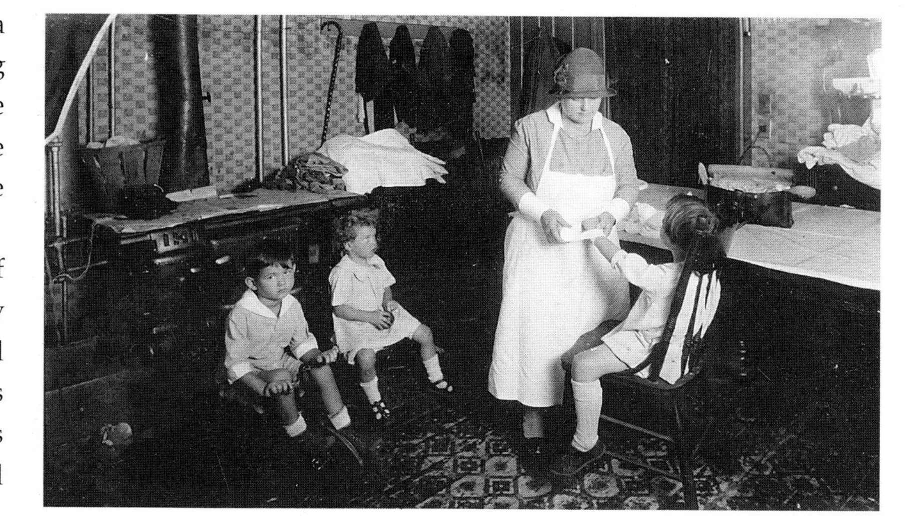

The Lancaster Visiting Nurses Association has been providing in-home health care to the county since 1908. Here, a nurse bandages the wrist of a young child as two others look on, circa 1926. LCHS D-02-02-43

Lydia Hamilton Smith, Stevens' housekeeper, also served as his confidante and was entrusted by the congressman with important missions. A black woman, she was a controversial figure in her day. Stevens had a noted artist paint her portrait.

General John Reynolds, a West Pointer recognized for his military astuteness, turned down the opportunity to lead the Union troops at Gettysburg. Shot by a sniper, he died on the first day of the battle that decided the outcome of the Civil War, sixty miles from his hometown.

The Patriot Daughters were among the first civilians to reach the war zone after the battle at Gettysburg. Rosina Hubley led the group in aiding the survivors. When the women ran out of bandages, they tore their petticoats into strips to bind wounds.

Dr. John L. Atlee was the first of that name to become a physician. He became president of the Pennsylvania Medical Society, helped organize the American Medical Association, and became its president in 1883. He and his brother Dr. Washington L. Atlee revived the practice of performing an ovariotomy despite the doubts of fellow surgeons. The patient lived a full lifetime.

Thomas Burrowes, of Strasburg, did well in public life until political changes sent him out of state government. He returned in 1836 with a new administration and through his work on behalf of education won the appellation of "father of public schools" in Pennsylvania.

These women busily fill Lancaster's photo needs. They worked in one of the photo processing laboratories of Darmstaetter's in 1930. LCHS D-10-04-11

James P. Wickersham founded the first Pennsylvania "normal school," or college to train teachers, in 1857. The school virtually closed down when most of its male students went off to fight in the Civil War, but the institution revived and is now Millersville University.

M. T. Garvin, born in 1860, was a farm boy who went to work early as an errand boy at the Fahnestock clothing firm in Lancaster, eventually rising to executive status. When his employer retired because of illness, Garvin took over and put the firm in his name, next to the courthouse on East King Street. His civic beneficence included restoration of the Old City Hall on Penn Square, now occupied by the Lancaster Cultural History Museum.

James Shand and Peter T. Watt worked together in Hartford, Connecticut, with Gilbert Thompson in the retail trade. They decided to start a shop in Lancaster in 1878. They bought out the interest of their deceased partner and opened in one small, thirty-by-sixty-foot room on Penn Square. It grew to become the Watt & Shand building, a present-day icon of downtown Lancaster.

Andrew Jackson Steinman bought the *Lancaster Intelligencer Journal* in 1866. His sons, Colonel J. Hale Steinman and John F. Steinman, expanded the business into Lancaster Newspapers, Inc., and pioneered into the emerging fields of radio and television.

Joseph F. Beiler, an Amish scholar, founded Pequea Publishers and originated *The Diary*, a monthly newsletter for fellow Amish members. He also published Amish directories and residence maps.

Mrs. Rusty Payne, a graduate of Wilberforce University, came to Lancaster in 1929 to become the first director of the newly organized Crispus Attucks Community Center. She stayed for three decades, serving at least two generations of Lancaster's African-American community.

Ruth Grigg Horting, of Lancaster, was the first woman to be appointed a member of a governor's cabinet in Pennsylvania. Having served in the state legislature, she was appointed Secretary of Public Welfare by Governor John S. Fine.

Hazel Dell Brown came to Lancaster as head of the newly created Bureau of Interior Design at Armstrong Cork Co., chosen by H. W. Prentiss Jr., the company's president. She became a nationally known and respected interior designer, a pioneer in designs of rooms for magazine photographs of Armstrong products.

Yetta Sachs Carpenter moved to Lancaster to manage the local shop of her sister, Mary Sachs, a women's apparel retailer. Yetta became known for her philanthropy.

Edna Schreiber was a registered nurse with an early interest in aiding children with physical disabilities. In 1936 she became the director of an organization to help polio victims, which later became affiliated with the Easter Seal Society. The Schreiber Pediatric Rehab Center is named in her honor.

Florence Starr Taylor was a prolific artist who created thousands of portraits and landscapes in watercolor, pastel, and other media. She is memorialized in a book of her Amish studies and a locally produced documentary.

Helen Reimensnyder Martin was an author whose novel, *Tillie, A Mennonite Maid*, created a sensation in the early 1900s. Some of her works were adapted for plays which did well on Broadway.

Herman F. Wohlsen came here from Germany in 1877 as a carpenter, and his satisfied

A group of kids gathers behind Kegel's Seafood Restaurant at 551 West King Street to watch William C. Myers' well drillers at work. At right, Bill Myers chats with Kenneth C. Myers, proprietor of Kegel's Produce.
LCHS 2-10-03-45

customers urged others to "get the Dutchman" to do their work because of his skill. The firm built such local structures as the old Woolworth Building, then the tallest structure in the city; the stable at the Williamson estate, now a residence and visible from the Lancaster County Historical Society's grounds; and the old Hotel Brunswick. Continuing with family involvement, Wohlsen Construction has broadened its market extensively.

Herbert Krone, in dark shirt, and three others work on a story for the *Lancaster New Era*, circa 1940. Krone was the *New Era*'s police reporter for many years.
LCHS 2-01-10-17

John K. Herr Jr. started making mattresses in 1907, working 59 hours a week with a staff of three. Now a major element in Serta, a federation of mattress manufacturers, it still relies on family participation.

In 1950 a group of four men—Henry Fisher, George Delp, Irl Daffin, and Raymond Buckwalter—bought the New Holland Machine Company (founded in 1895) to manufacture the world's first successful automatic pick-up, self-tying hay baler. The company's products are now sold worldwide.

Dutch Gold Honey was founded in 1946 by Ralph Gamber and his wife Luella after he suffered a heart attack and sought "a relaxing hobby." They bought three hives of bees for $27. Now the family-oriented business is the largest independent honey producer in the United States, packing more than 55 million pounds a year, with annual sales of $82.5 million.

Hazel I. Jackson was the first African-American woman to teach in the School District of Lancaster and at Millersville University. An annual memorial lecture now commemorates her contributions to the community.

INTO THE FUTURE

In the first decade of the twenty-first century, nearly 300 years after the first settlers clustered around Hans Herr's farm, about one of every two of the county's 480,000 inhabitants holds a paying job. Lancaster County's work ethic continues to power its efforts in all walks of life. The county is outstanding among all the counties of Pennsylvania for productivity and performance.

Its annual products are valued in billions of dollars, and it remains the Commonwealth's leader in agricultural production. On a given day, less than 3.8 percent of all its residents who can work are unemployed either by choice or by circumstance.

Customers around the world buy Lancaster County products and benefit from local businesses. Lancaster County commands international respect. And this has not come about merely by chance. People here not only work; they work at an infinite number of jobs for better products, better education, better health maintenance, and a better world. Their initiative, innovation, and insight are longstanding hallmarks of Lancaster at work.

During the 1920s traffic control at Penn Square consisted of a police officer like the one pictured here. He operated the semaphore signs, which directed drivers to stop or go. LCHS 1-04-01-18

REGULATOR
Time
your
Fixed
Shoes
For Sale
TITE

The Little Guys

John Ward Willson Loose

Lancaster County's economic health has long depended upon diversity. Major industries and thousands of small businesses all contribute to the county's financial well-being. The work ethic of Lancaster's businesspeople and their employees has been recognized nationwide and has brought many new companies and industries to the area. This variety of employment has kept Lancaster's economy relatively stable over the years.

Small businesses have ranged from sole proprietorships, such as shoemaker Ralph Ciccone, to family businesses, Frederick Gerlitzki's

continued…

Above: Theodora Valavanes stands behind the counter of her restaurant, Central Lunch, on West King Street, circa 1929. LCHS 2-10-02-45

Left: Domenic Lombardi ran his shoemaking and repair shop at 411 North Mary Street from about 1917 to 1930. "No loafing allowed in this shop," the sign read, and his employees were hard at work when the photographer stopped by in October, 1921. LCHS D-11-04-51

steeplejack and paint contracting, for example. The road to success traditionally involved hard work, long hours, a sense of service, and finding the right niche in Lancaster's economy. Even Hiram Kroome earned a decent living roaming Lancaster's city streets sharpening knives and scissors for anyone who desired his services.

With enough hard work and determination, smaller businesses flourished into larger successes. David Harnish's Lancaster Paint and Glass Company became a county fixture, serving Lancaster's painting needs for nearly 90 years. German immigrants' success at brewing beer turned Lancaster into a little Munich—until Prohibition took hold. What began in 1854 as Philip Lebzelter's Eagle Wheel and Bending Works is now the world's oldest dealer of Goodyear tires.

From bakeries and confectioneries to barber shops and oyster bars, Lancaster's small businesses have all added their contributions to the county's history. Collectively they have enriched a working-class tradition that carries on to this day.

The Gibbs Confectionery at 339 West Orange Street in Lancaster sold Ice Cream Puffs, two for a nickel, in 1900. George Gibbs opened the business during the 1890s, and his sons, Charles and Howard, carried on until about 1940. Gibbs' ice creams were known far and wide.
LCHS 1-01-03-26

Haefner's Brewery at Lime and Locust Streets contributed to the city's reputation of being "the Munich of the New World." Lancaster's many brewers used plain beer barrel wagons, not fancy rigs and teams of high-stepping Clydesdales.
LCHS D-10-05-90

When this photo was snapped in 1890, the Wenger Carriage Shop in Paradise had already been in business for more than thirty years. Elam Musser Bowman, a young carriage painter, is identified at the far right of this group of employees. LCHS 2-04-06-28

"This building is being painted by F. C. Gerlitzki contracting painter, steeplejack and rigger," advertised the sign on the balcony of the Wise Mansion on Manor Street. Frederick Gerlitzki made repairing the mansion a family affair. Fred Sr. hangs from the flagpole atop the house in this early 1920s photo. His son Joe stands on a ladder on the third floor. Sons Charles and Freddy Jr. perch on the second floor scaffolding, and daughters Grace, Emmy, and Margaret occupy the ladders below. LCHS 2-03-08-26

Surrounded by tobacco warehouses on North Prince Street, a hatless David Harnish is ready to supply house painters with linseed oil and white lead-based paint, circa 1900. Harnish's Lancaster Paint and Glass Company continued to meet Lancaster's painting needs until the store burned down in 1987. LCHS A-08-02-76

The mustachioed William Gerz awaits his next customer at his barber shop at 433 North Mulberry Street, circa 1910. Back when barbers shaved gentlemen in their shops, the customers' individual shaving mugs decorated the shelves. LCHS A-08-02-52

Philip Lebzelter's son, William, ran his own wagon wheel works in the 500 block of North Cherry Street in Lancaster for a short time. His employees took a break for a group portrait, circa 1895. LCHS 2-06-03-18

Lebzelter's got its start about 1854 as Philip Lebzelter's Eagle Wheel and Bending Works. By 1900 the company had adapted to servicing automobiles with Goodyear tires. Lebzelter's now ranks as the oldest Goodyear dealer in the world. Charles Lebzelter, David Reamer, and their employees posed for this early twentieth-century photograph at 241 North Queen Street in Lancaster. LCHS A-09-01-71

People considered Ralph Ciccone one of Lancaster's most skilled shoemakers. His busy shop, Ciccone & Co. Modern Shoe Repairing, occupied the southwest corner of Duke and Chestnut Streets in the 1920s. LCHS A-08-02-80

Hiram Kroome was quite the character around Lancaster. Pictured here in 1910 with the tools of his trade, Hiram sharpened his customers' scissors while humming a few bars of his favorite songs. LCHS 2-01-11-06

William R. Gamber and Wail al-Tikiriti hold honeycombs at Dutch Gold Honey in 1968. Al-Tikiriti came to the United States from Iraq to learn the honey-making trade. LCHS 2-10-02-51

When Samuel Tshudy (third from left) died in 1906, he'd been running his Oyster Bar & Saloon on West King Street for nearly twenty-one years. His establishment occupied the cellar of the old City Hall, now the Lancaster Cultural History Museum. In this photograph, taken about 1890, Samuel and his son, Joseph (fourth from left), stand ready to please the culinary tastes of Lancastrians. LCHS A-09-02-28

Lancaster's celebrated confectioneries employed many women in making and packaging their candies. These three ladies at the Jane Louise Candy Company on South Water Street demonstrate great willpower by not sampling the merchandise, circa 1950. LCHS A-10-02-25

Established in 1912 by brothers Samuel and Daniel Fichthorn and Ambrose Marburger, the F&M Hat Company of Denver continues to produce quality hats. This early photograph shows the men of the finishing room. Among the men identified from left are Robert Marburger, John Rupp, Harry Nelson, and Sam Seltzer. LCHS 2-10-02-79

Like many small businessmen, Elmer E. Brubaker relied on his truck, pictured here in 1939, to get him from service call to service call. Brubaker Electric, now Wilco Electric located near Columbia, was founded by Elmer Brubaker in 1937. LCHS 2-10-03-94

In 1913 H. K. Anderson bought the Eichler Bakery on North Christian Street, originally founded in 1889. He moved the company to Charlotte Street and renamed it the Anderson Pretzel Bakery. Today the company pumps out 4.5 million pretzels a week from its location on the Old Philadelphia Pike. These unidentified men twisted pretzels in the 1940s. LCHS 2-10-02-27

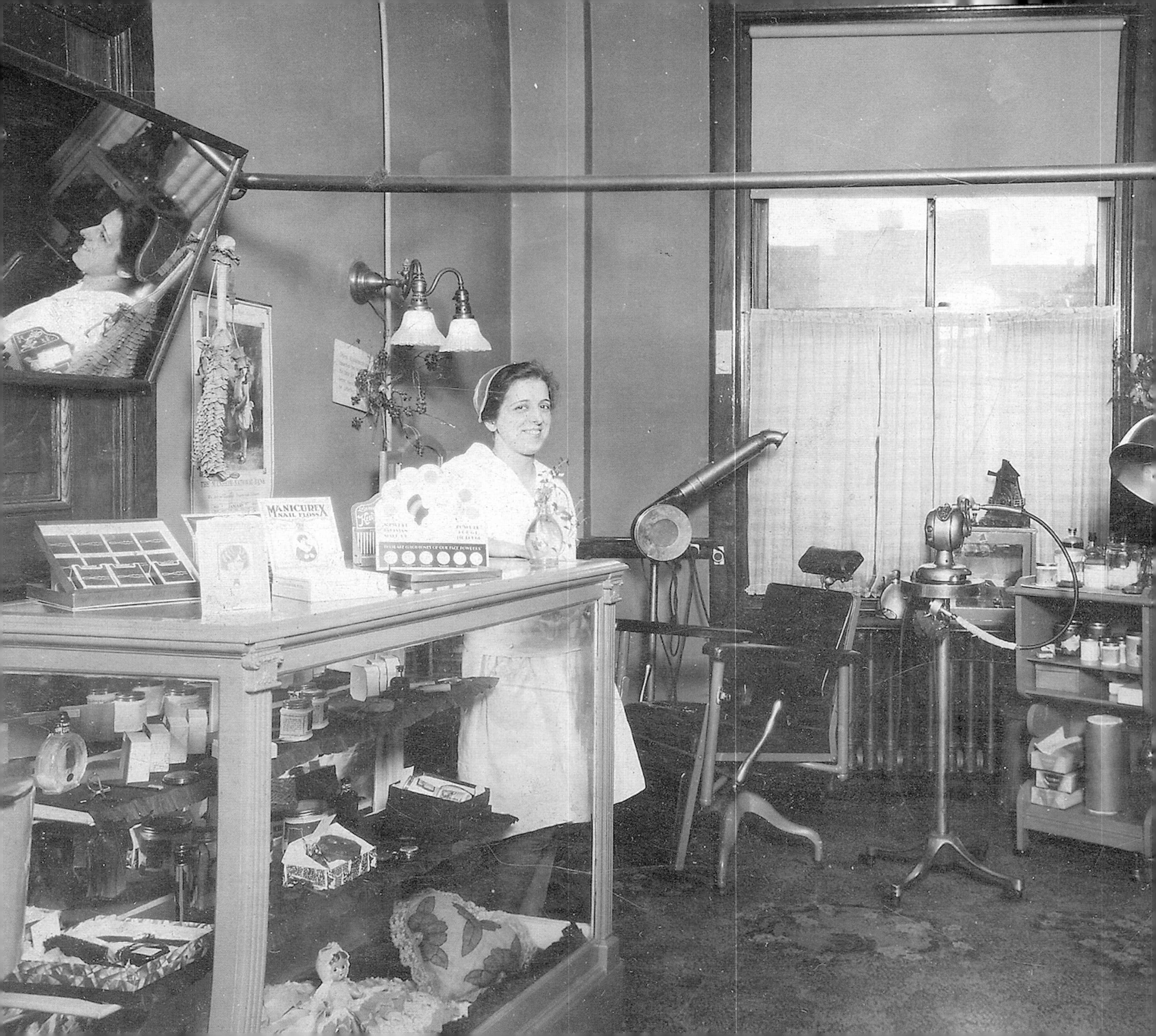
MANICUREX
NAIL FLOSS

A Woman's Work Is Never Done

Heather S. Tennies

In 1848, three hundred women and men signed the Declaration of Sentiments at a meeting held in Seneca Falls, New York. The declaration was a plea to end discrimination against women in all spheres of society, and it spearheaded the movement that led to women's suffrage, integrated juries, married women's property rights, minimum wage laws, and prohibitions against employment discrimination.

At the time, women in Lancaster owned and operated few businesses, but trade cards and newspaper advertisements do show female-owned establishments, including millinery and dress-making shops and an umbrella manufactory. Less than twenty percent of American women were employed outside the home in the nineteenth century. Most earned livings as teachers, nurses, midwives, domestic servants, and in factory and agricultural work.

Women began working in male-dominated professions by the early 1900s. The professions of law and medicine were more accessible to women, but many found positions as office workers, bond brokers, printers, and photograph processors. An increasing number of women owned and operated businesses, such as stores and beauty parlors. Female proprietors joined the local chamber of commerce and became active in improving their community through this organization, their churches, and benevolent societies.

continued...

Above: Two women identified only as Mollie and Lottie pluck feathers from chickens in preparation for the evening meal at what is now the Brethren Village Retirement Community, circa 1920. LCHS 2-10-02-42

Left: F. Ruth Hostetter opened her first beauty shop, Ye Quality Shoppe, in the Woolworth Building around 1925. She later ran this beauty shop in her home at 602 North Marshall Street. Originally from Manheim, Ms. Hostetter stayed in the business for several decades before passing away in 1982. LCHS 2-08-04-08

The employment rate of women reached thirty-six percent when businesses, including the Armstrong Cork Company, filled positions with female workers during World War II. Women gained experience in a variety of nontraditional jobs. They became welders, riveters, mechanics, electricians, and airplane builders on the home front, and they further contributed to the war effort by joining the Army and Navy. After V-J Day, the number of working women decreased as veterans returned to the work force.

When single and married women returned to work in the 1950s, they realized they had more career choices than were previously open to them. Sadly they had to wait until the 1960s to see the Equal Pay Act, the prohibition against employment discrimination in the Civil Rights Act, and an executive order prohibiting sex discrimination by government contractors.

The American work force has seen a steady increase in female employees since the 1960s. At present, more than one out of every four businesses is owned by a woman. Although it has not been an easy road, women now have successful careers in almost every field. The photographs on these pages depict only a small part of the working woman's journey through Lancaster County history.

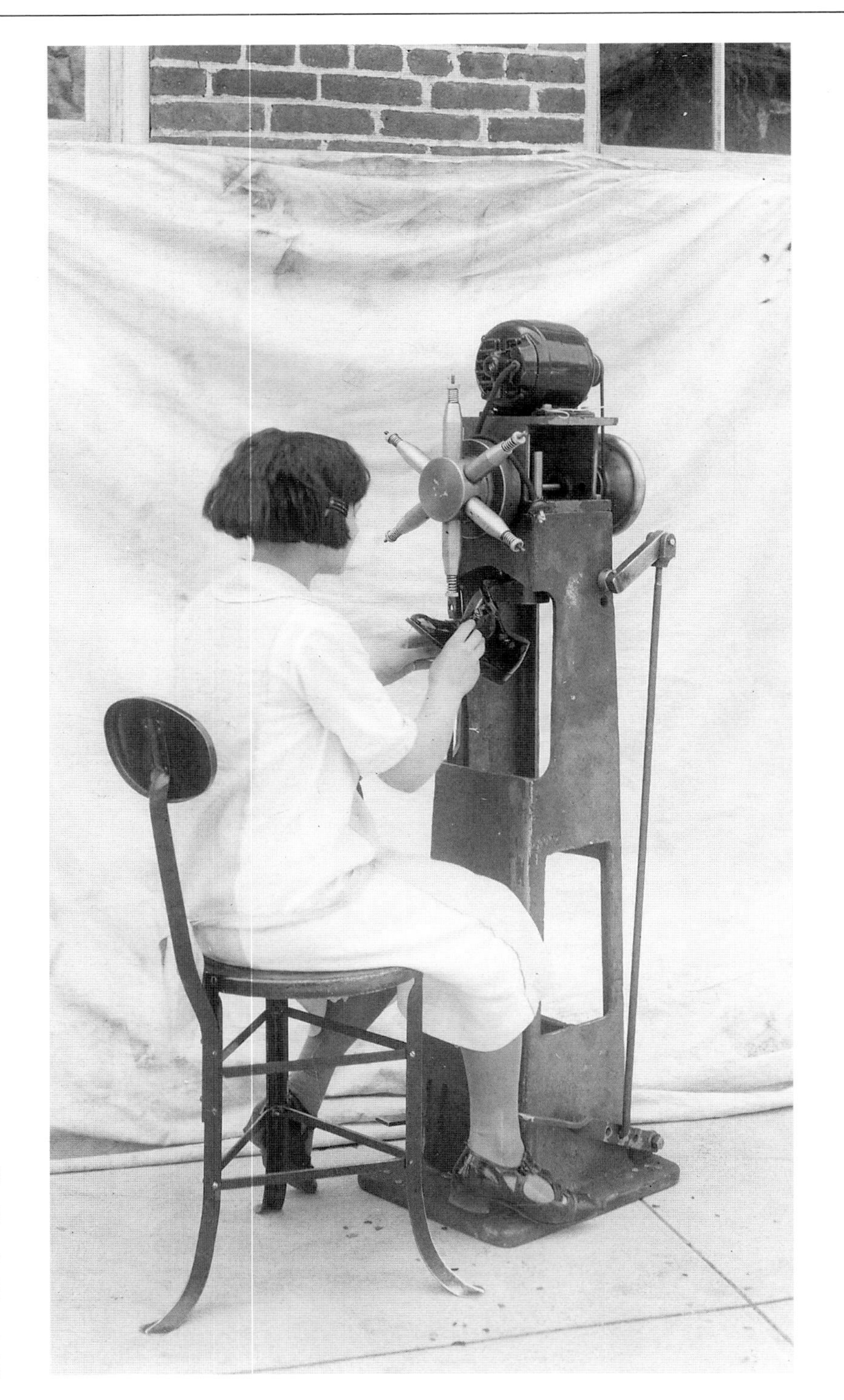

A young girl operates machinery of the Miller Hess Shoe Company in Akron, circa 1924. Peter B. Miller and Simon P. Hess founded the company around 1902. It closed its doors in 1984, and the building is now the home of the Mennonite Central Committee, at the corner of Main and Seventh Streets in Akron. LCHS D-11-01-64

Loretta Ganse Bowman, at left, and J. Frank Bowman pose with other employees of Bowman's cigar box factory in 1912. The factory burned down five years later. LCHS A-09-02-56

A kitchen employee works at the stove in Founders Hall at the Brethren Home of the Church of the Brethren, 1957. The business is now known as Brethren Village Retirement Community. LCHS 2-10-02-43

The women of the Welfare Federation prepare for a Community Chest Drive in November, 1925. The Welfare Federation was the predecessor of the United Way. The organization's offices were located in the Woolworth Building on North Queen Street. LCHS D-04-01-47

Right: An operator switches calls at the Bell Telephone Company of Pennsylvania, circa 1921. At the time of this photograph, Bell Telephone's offices and switchboards were located at 29–31 East Orange Street in Lancaster. The company moved to this location in 1908, having begun its existence in 1880 as the Pennsylvania Telephone Company based in Old City Hall on Penn Square. LCHS D-10-02-14

Above: Ladies work the Dial B Board at Bell Telephone Company of Pennsylvania, circa 1931. When this image was captured, the company had been operating out of its new location at 134 North Duke Street for about three years. The building is now City Hall. Bell Telephone remained in the building until the mid-1970s. LCHS D-10-02-34

The female employees of the Brunswick Hotel laundry service make sure the sheets are clean and pressed before returning them to use, 1926. A newer version of the hotel still stands at the corner of Queen and Chestnut Streets in Lancaster. LCHS D-10-02-90

The wait staff of the Hotel Brunswick sit for the photographer, 1927. In their neatly pressed uniforms, they provided the excellent service for which the hotel was known at the time. LCHS D-10-02-93

The Steinman Hardware Company's offices ran smoothly with the help of its female employees. Seen here in 1925, they kept the accounting in order, typed letters, and recorded orders. LCHS D-12-03-82

In 1930, women developed film and printed and trimmed photographs in the processing lab at Darmstaetter's store on North Queen Street. Darmstaetter's was the place to take your film for developing in Lancaster. LCHS D-10-04-07

Education was another field that initially provided employment for women. This woman, pictured in 1925, worked at New Holland High School. Note the large map of Lancaster County. LCHS D-12-05-40

Philadelphia-based G. H. P. Cigar operated a factory in Lancaster during the 1920s, manufacturing El Producto cigars, the stogie of choice of comedian George Burns. Pictured here are the ladies who made these fine cigars. Third and fifth from right, respectively, are Grace Bomberger and Stella Hutton. LCHS A-09-01-55

Are You Being Served?

Marianne Heckles

It all started with the dry goods store, so called because of the merchandise it sold: textiles, clothing, shoes. Some stores branched out and added bulk foods and hardware to their offerings. These "general stores" became the one-stop shopping centers of the nineteenth century. As the century progressed, the country grew, and so did the retail business. The dry goods store and general store would eventually evolve into the department store of today.

continued...

Above: Opened by William L. Bucher circa 1906, Bucher's Central Drug Store became a favorite hangout for the residents of Columbia. LCHS 1-01-03-55

Left: Holiday shoppers crowd into Steinman Hardware on West King Street in December, 1926. The store, now the site of the Pressroom Restaurant, was a city staple for hardware, sporting goods, and household items for decades. LCHS D-12-03-87

In Lancaster, Christopher Hager opened a dry goods store on West King Street in 1821. Hager's served several generations of citizens before closing its doors in 1977. In 1879, two new competitors arrived on the scene. Frank W. Woolworth opened his first successful five-and-dime store on Queen Street, and Watt & Shand's New York Store debuted on King Street.

Another Lancaster icon of its day, Darmstaetter's, grew out of a profitable photo supply business. The store expanded to sell household appliances and even boats in addition to their camera equipment. Specialty stores selling specific clothing items, such as hats, shoes, or jewelry, popped up throughout the county as the demand for them grew.

Hardware stores were also an offshoot of the old dry goods store. Steinman's Hardware on West King Street sold everything from tools to sporting goods to camping gear. Now the site of the Pressroom Restaurant, Steinman's existed as a hardware store for more than 200 years, making it one of America's oldest such retail operations.

Today, outlet malls help attract throngs of tourists to Lancaster County. After all, everyone needs a little retail therapy (and a bargain) every now and then. With the abundance of businesses that have graced the area during the last two centuries, it's no wonder Lancaster is one happy county.

Frank W. Woolworth, left, stands in front of his first store on North Queen Street, circa 1880. The young man at right may be Charles Hoffmeier, who began working in Woolworth's store when he was fifteen years old. LCHS D-12-04-74

Groff and Wolf men's store satisfied men's clothing needs for generations of Lancastrians. Groff and Wolf's sold everything from Golden Arrow collars to Boy Scout uniforms. In 1930, their window showcase advertised starched or soft collars for 35 cents apiece or three for a dollar. LCHS D-10-05-74

Douglas, Adolph, and Harcourt Darmstaetter pose for a snapshot with their employees at the store's photography counter. Note the ad in the background for the Amateur Cinema Club meeting at the Grubb Mansion in Musser Park on January 27, probably 1954. LCHS D-10-03-84

Proving that Darmstaetter's met all household needs, this 1934 store window showed off their fine selection of lamps, irons, toasters, waffle irons, wringer washers, ice boxes, and even photo developing and picture framing services.
LCHS D-10-04-31

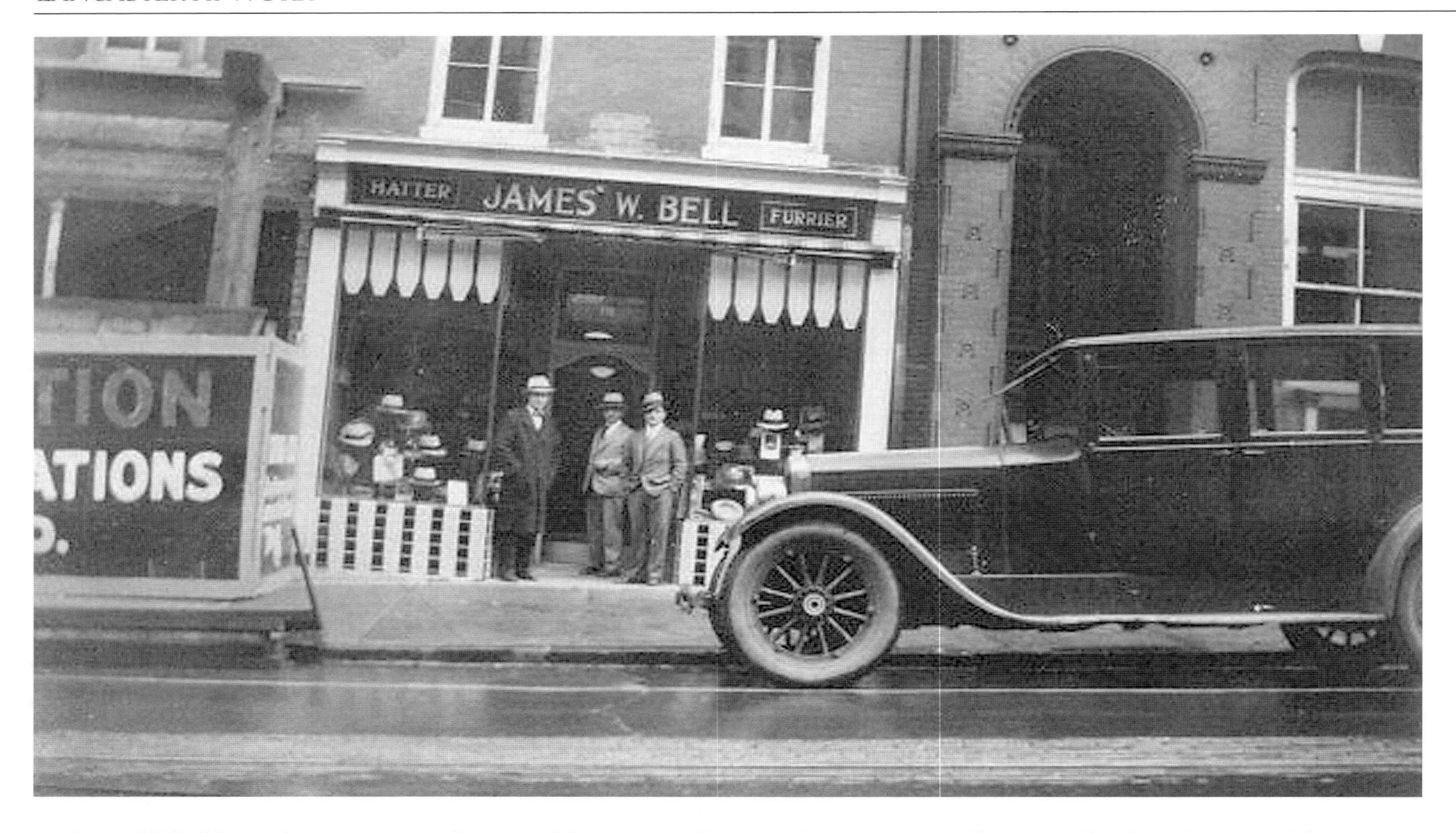

James W. Bell began his business as a hatter and furrier at 15 West King Street circa 1920. The store offered the finest men's hats, including Stetsons, and also sold, stored, dressed, repaired, and remodeled furs until closing its doors in the mid-1970s.
LCHS 1-01-03-20

When it closed in the late 1970s, Hager's was one of the nation's oldest department stores. Founded by Christopher Hager in 1821, the store operated in the first block of West King Street. LCHS 2-06-01-23

For thirty years Return E. Fahnestock operated his dry goods store next to the courthouse on East King Street. Upon Fahnestock's death in 1895, Milton T. Garvin took over the store, which later became Garvin's Department Store. Pictured in front of Fahnestock's in 1893 are, from left, Calvin Weidle, Milton T. Garvin, Edwin T. Piersol, and Jacob Hupper. LCHS 2-06-01-20

Pictured circa 1900, Israel Doster ran this dry goods store at 48–52 East Main Street in Lititz from about 1897 until his death in 1950. LCHS 3-02-01-09

In 1925, manager Ella Miller, left, and her three clerks, Anne Mae Erisman, Ruby Driver, and Margaret Howard, prepare for another day's sales at the Gross Millinery Store on East King Street. LCHS A-08-01-23

In 1915, Harry Dietz's Shoe Store advertised "soft shoes for tender feet." Dietz's store was in business at 63 North Queen Street from about 1913 to 1931. LCHS D-10-04-46

W. Scott Leinbach opened his "daylight department store"—so called because of the store's tremendous skylights—at 47–49 North Queen Street about 1895. American flags and bunting adorned the store in 1930, possibly for Veteran's Day. LCHS D-11-04-18

This display of ladies' undergarments in M. T. Garvin's store window was a bit racy by 1930's standards. Garvin's store stood next to the courthouse on East King Street. LCHS D-10-05-46

L. B. Herr began his career selling books and stationery in the 1880s. By 1911 he was filling all of Lancaster's office supply needs from his store at 46–48 West King Street. A photographer from Darmstaetter's snapped this window display in 1929.
LCHS D-11-01-47

John H. Sensenig owned and operated this jewelry store in New Holland during the early part of the 1900s. Here, a young man sizes up a new pocket watch. LCHS D-12-02-65

Marianne Heckles

In 1879, three young entrepreneurial Scotsmen—Peter Watt, Gilbert Thompson, and James Shand—bought the stock and building of the New York Store at 20–22 East King Street in Lancaster. In short order, the company became known as Watt & Shand's New York Store. (Thompson had died.) It quickly made a good business out of serving the fashion needs of Lancaster's citizens.

A year after their opening, Watt & Shand moved their business a few doors down the street to 8–10 East King Street, and the store grew rapidly. In 1885, the company bought out the neighboring Gerhart Clothing Store, and ten years later, it purchased the former Prangley Building on the corner of Penn Square. By 1903, Watt & Shand had replaced the Prangley Building with a grand four-story structure designed by noted Lancaster architect Cassius Emlen Urban.

Watt & Shand soon became a full-service department store, offering men's and women's clothing, shoes, furs, household items, and even a soda fountain. The soda fountain, in later days called the Rendezvous, served as a location for many a first date, after-school snacks, and lunches with friends.

The store was notorious for its sales promotions, well-decorated store windows, and gimmicky traditions, including the arrival of Santa Claus each holiday season. During the 1950s and 1960s, children flocked downtown on the Saturday after Thanksgiving to see Santa arrive on a fire

continued…

Left: Pictured here circa 1930, the shoe department at Watt & Shand offered a full line of ladies' shoes. LCHS A-09-01-87

Above: Watt & Shand's New York Store moved from its original location at 20–22 East King Street to this spot at 8–10 East King Street in 1880, just a year after opening for business. LCHS A-09-01-89

truck. They watched as he climbed up the ladder to Watt & Shand's fourth floor.

Continuing the expansion theme of its early days, Watt & Shand acquired the Appel and Weber Jewelry Store and their local competition, Hager's, by 1970. The company also opened a full-service department store at the newly built Park City Center.

With the mall location providing more parking and convenience, sales at the downtown store declined. In 1992, department store chain The Bon-Ton bought out Watt & Shand. Although the mall location remains in business today, the downtown store closed in 1995, bringing an end to a Lancaster shopping landmark.

Top: Picking out the prettiest dress was no easy task for these ladies in the pattern department, circa 1950. LCHS WS-01-01-42

Bottom: Perhaps the fondest memories of Watt & Shand are of icy cold sodas and Texas Tommy hot dogs at the Rendezvous, the store's soda fountain, seen here in the 1920s. LCHS WS-01-01-33

A brave Santa climbs the ladder of a fire truck to Watt & Shand's fourth floor, signalling the start of the holiday season.
LCHS WS-01-01-11

The Watt & Shand department store grew to dominate the southeast corner of Penn Square. A photo, circa 1898, (top, right) shows the first piece of the now familiar facade in place. Just to the left is the store's second location, shown in more detail on page 59. LCHS A-09-01-42

In the photo below, taken April 8, 1926, the last holdout on the South Queen Street corner is being demolished to complete the store's presence on Penn Square. LCHS WS-01-01-37

At far right, a circa 1938 photo shows a crowd of shoppers gathering at the store's entrance as trolley cars, trucks, and automobiles swirl around the Soldiers and Sailors Monument. One final section remained to be built between the southern end of the store on South Queen Street and the three-and-a-half story Montgomery House, visible on the right edge of the photo. LCHS WS-01-01-26

WATT
&
SHAND
WATT & SHAND
WATT & SHAND
WATT & SHAND

From Farm to Market

Linda S. Aleci

"As we leave Chester County…the great county of Lancaster, in all its glory, expands before the eye…. It is, without a doubt, the garden of this glorious Union, and there are few spots in this wide world, which could present a nobler scene to the eye than is here afforded…. The whole of the country is in the highest state of cultivation; and in the economy which characterizes the general agricultural system, there is probably not a more prolific region in the United States."

—Eli Bowen, *The Pictorial Sketchbook of Pennsylvania*

The conditions Eli Bowen described in 1853 essentially set Lancaster's course well into the twentieth century. The "gift of good land" and the labors of those who carried it from farm to market built an economy that linked Lancaster's urban and rural peoples, giving shape to the region's towns and villages and defining its near-legendary identity.

The hub of this network was the city of Lancaster. Now America's last surviving market town, it was organized around the typical configuration of a central market square, courthouse, and public offices. This footprint quickly expanded as food retailing and processing establishments were incorporated into the urban fabric. Many of Lancaster's most distinctive and significant structures—the grand Victorian market houses, the corner groceries dotting the neighborhoods, the tobacco warehouses, breweries, mills, and granaries that were

continued…

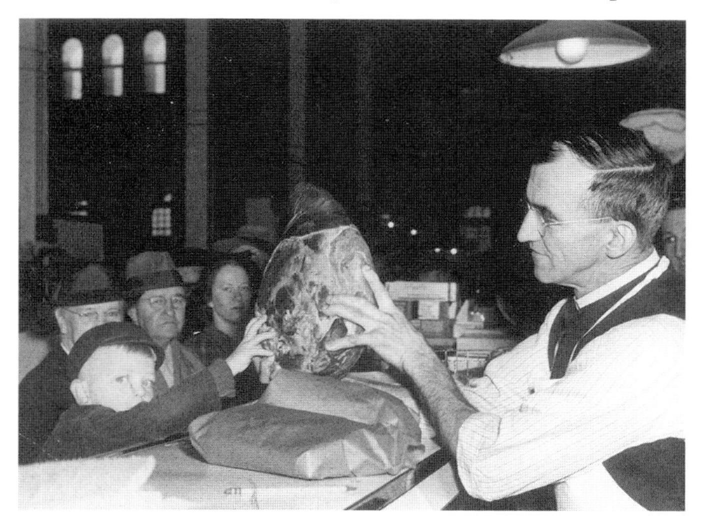

Above: Jacob H. Thomas sells an Easter ham to three-year-old Billy Hess at Central Market in 1946. LCHS A-09-03-08

Left: A farmer near Washington Boro takes a break from driving his horse-drawn binder, circa 1917. LCHS D-08-01-94

fed by rail lines running into the city—are the legacy of the journey from field to table and beyond.

Inclined to small-scale farming owing both to culture and topography, Lancaster's agrarian economy remained strong for a number of reasons. Proximity to burgeoning urban centers helped keep agricultural production diverse, entrepreneurial, and comparatively resistant to recession. City populations offered new opportunities for commercial agriculture—tobacco and dairy farming—as well as truck-farming and other smaller-scale enterprises that served the household.

These photographs, mostly taken during the early twentieth century, also record the demand for the new and exotic, with pineapples and bananas nestling alongside peaches and melons—a sign of larger shifts in the nation's foodways.

Rohrer's Med-O-Farms Dairy manufactured "tuberculin tested and pasteurized milk and cream," according to the advertisement in the 1931 Lancaster City Directory. Seen here in 1930, employees at the dairy in Bridgeport inspect bottles of milk before they are delivered to customers. LCHS D-12-02-12

Pictured here in June of 1896 is William N. Matter's grocery store at 522 North Duke Street. Mr. Matter ran the store until about 1910. LCHS 2-03-07-21

Arthur S. Young and Company of Kinzers repaired this farmer's tractor and equipment about 1925. LCHS D-08-01-93

More than 5,000 people gathered for the First Annual Fat Stock Show and Auction at the Union Stock Yards on June 1 and 2, 1921. Lancaster's Union Stock Yards were once the largest stockyards east of Chicago. Today, the remains of the once thriving business, located along Lititz Pike and Marshall Avenue just north of Lancaster City, are slated for redevelopment. LCHS A-08-01-66

The John W. Eshelman & Sons Feed Mill served the county for many decades, beginning around 1895. Today its site at 238–246 North Queen Street is occupied by the Susquehanna Association for the Blind and Vision Impaired.
LCHS A-09-01-47

Mailroom employees prepare orders at the American Seed Company in 1920. The bulk of the company's sales came from schoolchildren selling packets of seeds door to door. Established in or about 1920, American Seed's offices were last located at Prince and Grant Streets in Lancaster, now the site of a parking lot. LCHS D-10-01-25

Smoking was not allowed in the A. H. Hoffman Seed Company's warehouse in Landisville. Note the drying corn cobs hanging from the ceiling in this photograph, taken circa 1921. LCHS D-11-01-72

Robert Renninger's Duke Street Meat Market provided many Lancastrians with quality meats. Located at 9 North Duke Street, the market operated from circa 1920 to about 1966. Picture here in 1921, two butchers show off a few prime cuts. LCHS D-12-01-93

The women of the Keystone Pecan Company in Manheim shell pecans in 1927. LCHS D-11-02-92

Sunshine Biscuits and Florida grapefruit were just a few of the foods offered at Robert Seldomridge's grocery store at 42 West King Street. The store operated during the 1920s and 1930s. LCHS D-12-02-64

It's opening day of the Grand Union Company, July 17, 1931. The store, located at 141 North Queen Street, stayed in business only a few years. LCHS D-10-05-68

Simon Leapman and his family operated their grocery store at 843 North Queen Street for nearly forty years, until Simon's death in 1940. The employees pictured here in 1925 await their next patron. LCHS D-11-04-15

Musser's market stand sells the finest meats, butter, and cheeses, circa 1921. LCHS D-11-04-75

From left, James Lenox, Paul Checkley, and two unidentified employees get the Royal Fruit Market near King and Duke Streets ready for another day's business in 1935. James Lenox and Earl Kegel were the produce business's proprietors. LCHS A-08-01-12

Eli S. Garber opened what would become Penn Dairies, Inc., in Stevens in 1890. Pictured here in front of the Second Street bottling plant are the company's milk deliverymen and salesmen, circa 1932. LCHS A-08-01-77

Men inspect large 40-quart cans at the Lancaster Sanitary Milk Company, circa 1920. The company, which later became part of Penn Dairies, Inc., occupied the southwest corner of Frederick and Queen Streets in Lancaster. LCHS D-12-02-42

Top: Proud farmhands show off their tobacco crop at Mr. Fondersmith's farm, July 20, 1895. LCHS 2-04-04-31

Bottom: Workers gather tobacco in the fields at Lime Spring Farm in Rohrerstown, circa 1955. LCHS S-01-08-27

Barry R. Rauhauser

Sometime between 1997 and 2002, one of Lancaster's long-held traditions passed away. The Agricultural Census of 2002 recorded the epilogue to this chapter of the area's cultural history.

Tobacco was no longer Lancaster County's premier cash crop.

Discovered in America and transported around the world, tobacco has always been a part of Lancaster County's history. First opened in 1770, Lancaster's Demuth Tobacco Shop remains America's oldest continually operating tobacco shop. The term "stogie" originated in Lancaster—a nickname for the long cigars smoked by westward traveling wagon masters aboard their Conestoga wagons. As early as 1828, some Lancaster County farmers chose to grow their own crops of tobacco rather than pay a dear price for imports. By 1839, Lancaster County topped all Pennsylvania counties in tobacco production.

Growing and harvesting tobacco for cigars was incredibly labor intensive. Local Amish and Mennonite communities favored the crop, as their work ethic and labor force matched tobacco's demanding nature. Representatives from American Cigar, Swisher, and Bayuk Cigar made pilgrimages to Lancaster County to scour Amish farms for the highest quality leaf. Tobacco farming reached its peak of 35,000 acres in the late 1950s, with Lancaster producing 90 percent of Pennsylvania's crop.

After this peak, Lancaster's tobacco production steadily declined, a result of increasing competition, changes in tobacco preferences, and changes in technological production of smoking

products. Tobacco still remained king of the crops in terms of market value, but much of it was used for cigarettes and smokeless tobacco products rather than cigars. By the 1990s, tobacco grew on less than 10,000 acres of county farmland.

Over the past ten years, the number of farms and the amount of farmland devoted to tobacco has declined by more than fifty percent, a national trend spurred by the changing cultural acceptance of tobacco usage. In 2002, for the first time, the total market value of tobacco produced in Lancaster was exceeded by other harvested commodities, such as grains, vegetables, and nursery products. Flowers and potted plants dethroned the once mighty tobacco.

Top: Bundles of freshly rolled cigars abound at the G. H. P. Cigar Company factory in the 1920s. LCHS 2-10-02-94

Bottom: Charles S. Brenneman's Leaf Tobacco Company warehouse, seen here in 1920, still stands at the corner of Walnut and Plum Streets in Lancaster. Today it's the home of the Lancaster Brewing Company. LCHS D-10-02-64

The Office

Marianne Heckles

Scribes have existed since the invention of writing, but they didn't have offices as we know them until the turn of the twentieth century. With rapid industrial expansion, big business took off, increasing the need for clerical and other desk-based jobs. Corporate America began to grow into the maze of cubicles so prevalent today. The expansion of government in the late 1900s helped provide a wealth of new white-collar jobs.

continued...

Above: A reporter writes his story for tomorrow's newspaper at the *New Era and Examiner* offices on North Queen Street in October, 1920. The newsroom moved to its present location on West King Street in 1929. LCHS D-11-05-58

Left: Female staffers busily type in the offices of the Lancaster Business College, circa 1921. The college was located at 48 North Queen Street. LCHS D-01-03-10

Whether you call them pencil pushers or desk jockeys, office occupants come in many varieties. They include bank tellers, accountants, secretaries, administrators, lawyers, reporters, insurance agents, and many other occupations. The office is their home, forty hours a week, whether in a corner suite in the Griest Building or a cubicle in a suburban office park.

Certainly office technology has changed over time, even if the tasks performed have not. While our clerical ancestors dealt with typewriters and carbon paper instead of computers and laser printers, they, too, provided administrative services. They kept the invoices filed, the books balanced, the reports written, the staff assisted, and the clients happy.

Lancaster County is no different. From the county courthouse to the newsroom, from school district offices to the headquarters of the many industries rooted here, office buildings hum with the sounds of photocopiers and fax machines, computers, telephones, and the gurgle of water coolers and coffee machines.

The office worker may not create a sellable product like the blue-collar laborer does, but the office worker provides services that are just as essential. From file clerks to the steno pool to the receptionist and even the boss, all are important to a smoothly functioning office and a growing corporate world ever more geared toward a service economy.

A woman at the Union Savings Systems office at 20 East Chestnut Street proudly shows off her work in 1921.
LCHS D-12-04-17

Lancaster's superintendent of schools, Robert K. Buehrle, takes a break from his day to pose for the photographer, circa 1890. His office was located in the city's high school at 237 West Orange Street. The gas lamp on his desk and the phone on the wall were relatively advanced furnishings for the time. LCHS A-08-03-14

Another day at the Register of Wills office at the Lancaster County Courthouse, circa 1914. Pictured from left are Christian F. Stoner, deputy register; B. Frank Musser, clerk; Howard Paules, janitor; and John Redsecker and Charles Strickler, clerks.
LCHS 2-03-05-28

Sheets of copy await perusal by the employees of the New Era Printing Company in March, 1902. Seated from left are copy holder Boyd Maxwell and proofreaders William Zecher, Oliver Smith, and Burch Kieffer. LCHS 2-03-06-22

Election night is a hectic time at any newspaper office. Here, staffers at the *Intelligencer Journal* office anxiously take down poll results as they are phoned in on election night, November 2, 1920. The next day's headline read,"Harding Elected President in Big Sweep; Republicans Gain in the House and Senate; Lancaster Gives Big Lead to GOP Forces." LCHS D-11-02-15

Linotypers at the *Examiner*'s printing office get the day's copy ready for the presses, circa 1920. LCHS D-11-05-64

Guy Smeltz, secretary of the Keystone Pecan Company in Manheim, at work in November, 1927. Elam G. Hess founded the company in 1912 when he bought several pecan orchards near Albany, Georgia. The business was later called Pecano, after a type of pecan flour the company produced. LCHS D-11-02-94

The Lancaster Ministerial Association and Teachers' Protective Union, led by Rev. E. A. Bawden and Rev. James W. Meminger, kept offices at 226 East Orange Street. These gentleman get caught up on their paperwork, circa 1914. LCHS D-11-05-19

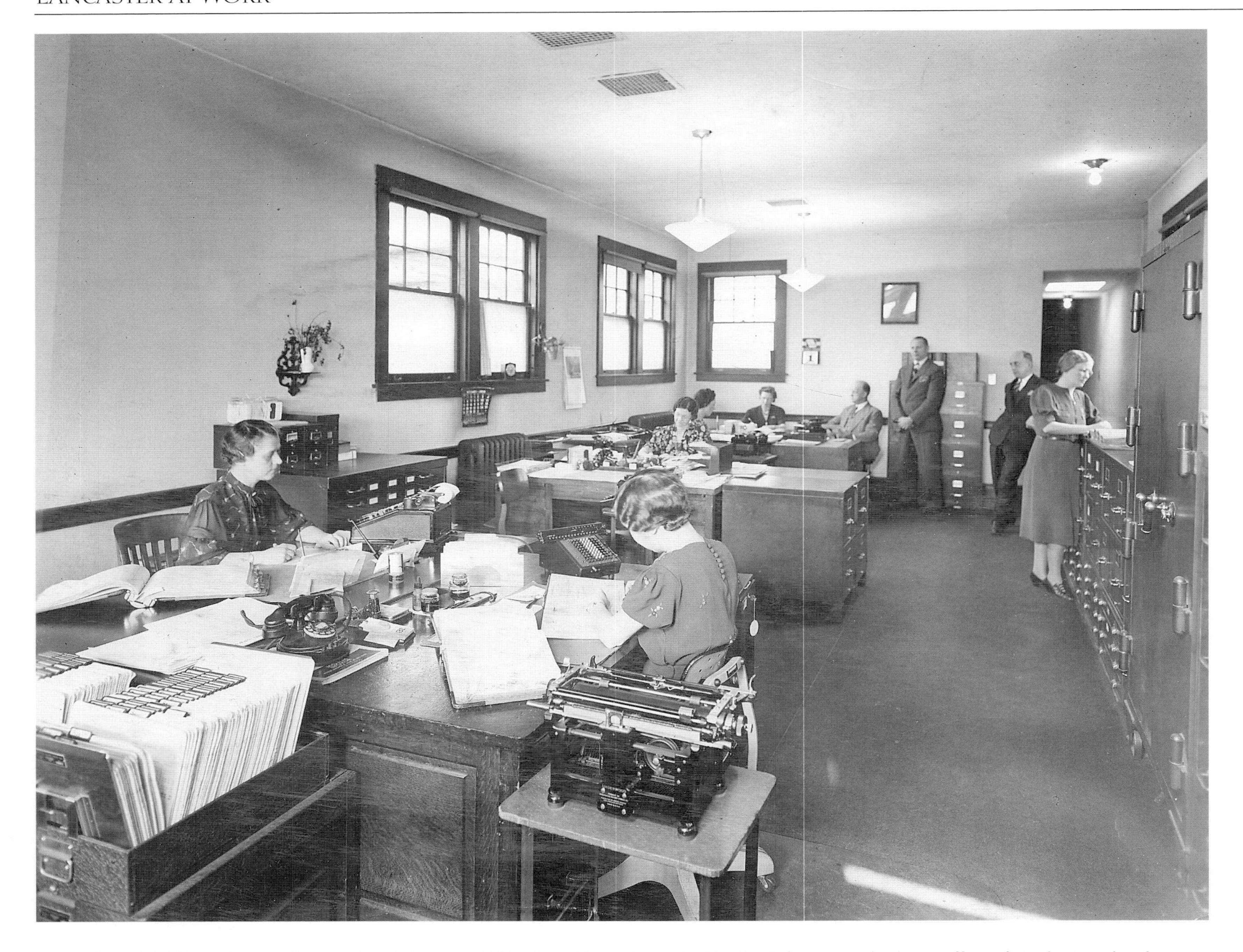

Robert F. McMurtrie, standing under picture, and Christian G. Engle, seated to the left, survey the busy office of Engle-Hambright and Davies, circa 1938. The local insurance and real estate agency opened for business in 1896. LCHS 2-10-02-72

The office of the Goodville Mutual Casualty Company hums with activity in the 1930s. A small group of Mennonite men started the company in 1926 to meet the growing need for automobile insurance in Lancaster County. LCHS 2-10-03-18

The employees of Wayne L. Rohrer's Med-O-Farms Dairy near Bridgeport didn't have time to pause for the photographer in 1930. LCHS D-12-02-13

Employees at Ephrata National Bank await customers, circa 1918. Identified from left are William M. Irwin, J. Harry Hibshman, Wayne K. Martin, Martin L. Weidman, and Clarence J. Raezer. LCHS 2-10-02-71

Blue-Collar Lancaster

William E. Krantz

In the eighteenth and early nineteenth centuries, industries in Lancaster County served the needs of the local area. Flour mills, sawmills, buggy makers, and tinsmiths each employed only a few people. Their raw materials and their customers came from nearby locations. The numerous clockmakers and furniture makers produced their wares one piece at a time, often to fill a specific order. Practical transportation was not available to send their products to faraway markets.

The advent of railroads and canals in the 1840s made it possible to bring in large quantities of raw materials and ship finished goods to regional and even national markets. These new economic resources led to the eventual growth of large factories employing many people. Companies based in Lancaster could advertise and sell their branded products on a national scale.

The demise in the first half of the 1900s of cotton and silk mills, both large employers, was offset by the growth of new industries. Armstrong Cork Company, Hamilton Watch Company, and Radio Corporation of America (RCA) built large manufacturing plants in Lancaster. During World War II, all three assisted the nation by converting part of their manufacturing capabilities to produce military products. R. R. Donnelly & Sons, printers,

continued...

Above: Employees of the Lancaster Concrete Tile Company form tiles by hand, 1920. The company was located at 234 North Water Street in Lancaster. LCHS D-11-03-46

Left: Early in the twentieth century, the Lancaster Iron Works built a plant for fabricating structural steel products along South Water Street, north of Seymour Street. Later, with the acquisition of the Henry Martin Brickmaking Machine Co., another erecting shop and foundry were built off of Harrisburg Pike at the end of Race Avenue. About this time the Posey family took over the company. This 1920 photo shows the boiler and pressure vessel shop employees. LCHS 3-18-01-02

and New Holland Machine Company, manufacturers of farm machinery, also established plants in Lancaster County, where thousands of Lancastrians worked in the latter half of the twentieth century.

The county is now home to 1,250 smaller factories employing more than 46,000 people. That translates to about one tenth of the county's population. Lancaster County companies manufacture furniture and wood products, malleable iron and structural steel, and other metal products. We make candy, cereal, cheese, ice cream, meat, and other food items. Even high tech products unknown only a few years ago now come out of Lancaster County.

The skills and dedication of every worker who designed, built, sold, or delivered anything ever manufactured in Lancaster County have contributed to the long-term health of the area's economy. It is, in part, their work ethic for which the county has come to be recognized across the nation.

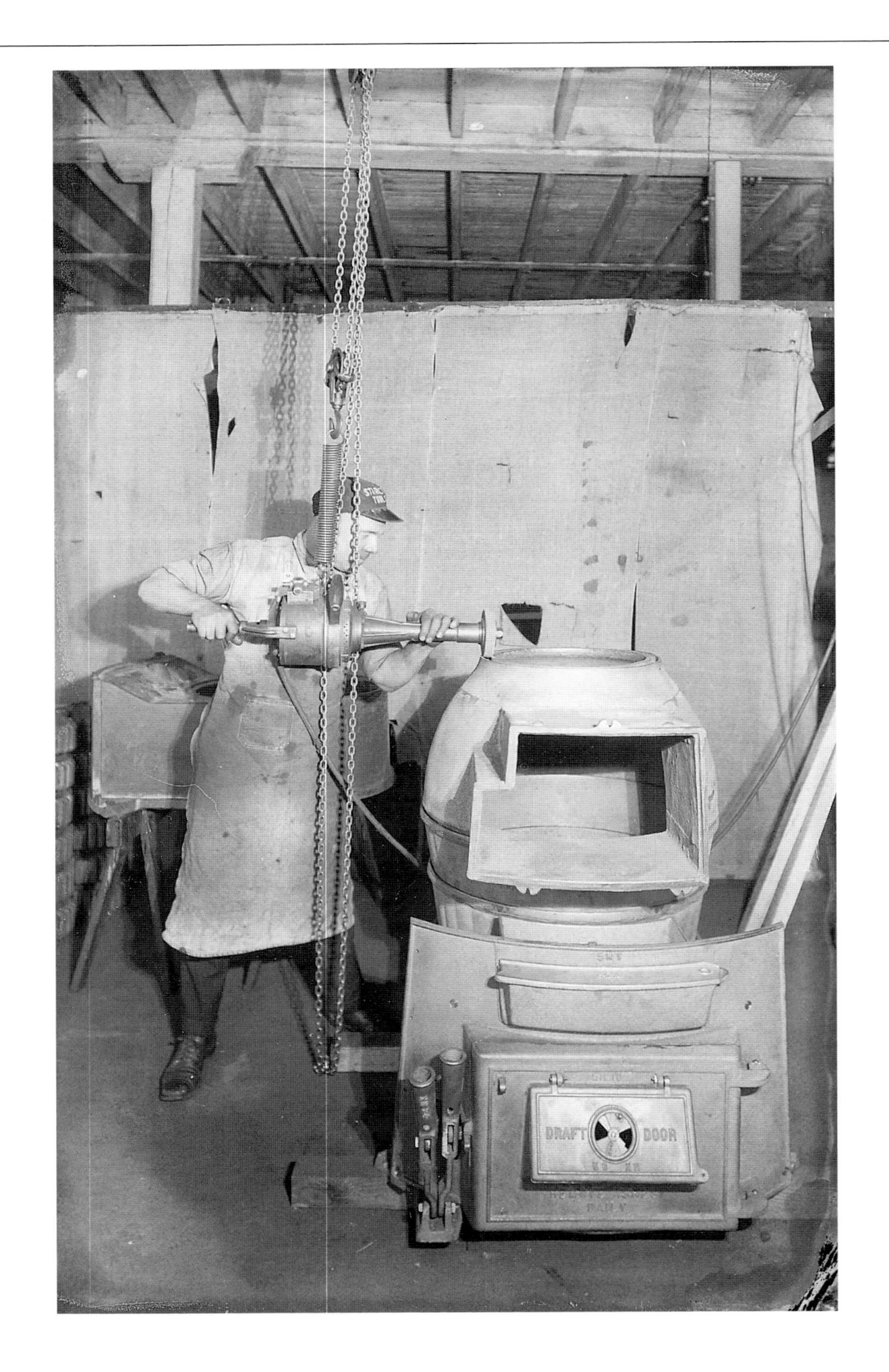

Founded in 1895 as the New Holland Machine Works, New Holland has grown into a worldwide corporation famous for its top-of-the-line agricultural machinery. The man pictured here in 1926 is grinding a hot-air-furnace shell. LCHS D-11-05-78

Gustavus Groezinger's tannery on South Water Street was not a pleasant place to work, thanks to the smell, but it provided employment for Lancaster's men and boys during its many decades of operation. The tannery was located along Hoffman's Run, which gave Water Street its name. LCHS 2-01-01-18

Above: Employees tend to the looms at the Stehli Silk Mill, circa 1920. Stehli Silks Corporation, a Swiss company, built its sprawling plant in Lancaster in the 1890s. The mill ceased operations in 1954. LCHS D-12-03-61

Right: Lancaster's Stehli Silk Mill, the longest silk weaving mill building in the nation, stretched 900 feet along Martha Avenue. The Stehli family always landscaped their textile mills to be attractive sites. This 1931 aerial photo shows the superintendent's home in the lower left corner and the Pennsylvania Railroad tracks in back of the mill. LCHS 2-06-03-21

Tool- and die-makers toil away in the machine shop at the Hamilton Watch Company, circa 1910. Note the overhead power transmission shafting and belt-driven machinery. LCHS 2-06-04-03

Marianne Heckles

In 1875, the Adams & Perry Watch Manufacturing Company became the first in a succession of local watch-making businesses that failed. Adams & Perry, the Lancaster Watch Company, and the Keystone Standard Watch Company all came and went during the next fifteen years.

And then came Hamilton Watch. Organized in 1892 with capital from some of Lancaster's most prominent citizens, the Hamilton Watch Company took its name from the city's founding fathers, Andrew and James Hamilton. The company geared itself to produce high-quality timepieces.

Almost immediately, railroad employees hailed the watches for their precision. Hamilton began advertising its products as "the Railroad Timekeeper of America" and "the Watch of Railroad Accuracy." By the early twentieth century, Hamilton was keeping a growing nation running on time.

In 1914, a Hamilton watch kept the dirt-moving trains in synch during the construction of the Panama Canal. The 1928 New York Yankees received commemorative championship Hamilton watches. Everyone from the average Joe to Babe Ruth wore a Hamilton.

With World War II looming on the horizon, the company switched gears to help out the war effort. They began production of time fuses for artillery shells and special timepieces for aviation and naval navigation. During the war, the company became known for its Hamilton Marine Chronometer, an instrument used by ships at sea for precise navigation.

After the war, the company focused on making fashionable timepieces for every type of person. Hamilton even went Hollywood: Elvis Presley wore a Ventura model Hamilton watch during 1961's *Blue Hawaii*, and director Stanley Kubrick commissioned the company to make watches and clocks for 1966's *2001: A Space Odyssey*. The company went from a national to an international sensation in the decades after the war.

In 1972, Hamilton brought watch technology to a new level with the introduction of the digital watch. The company has undergone many changes and mergers since then. Hamilton watches are still produced by the Swatch Group, a Swiss company. Bulova Technologies, now L3 Communications, continues Hamilton's defense production work in Lancaster County.

Top right: Microscopic precision ensures the quality of Hamilton Watch's products, circa 1920. LCHS 2002.091.54

Bottom right: Built in 1875, this factory on Columbia Avenue served as the home of Hamilton Watch until the building was sold in 1981 to become the Clock Tower Apartments. LCHS 1-01-03-21

Machinists at the Hershey Foundry and Machine Company in Manheim produce castings for motor stokers, the company's best known product, in 1928. The company's motor stoker fed coal automatically into furnaces and boilers and dropped the ash into a bin. It was a welcome invention both for commercial and domestic heating in the early twentieth century. LCHS D-11-01-59

Workers at the Pennsylvania Soap Company shovel fat particles to be processed into soap, 1926. Founded by Herman Miller in the 1840s as the Miller Soap Company, the company became the Pennsylvania Soap Company about 1900. The company ceased operation in 1933. LCHS D-12-01-23

Bench molders work in the foundry of the Columbia Malleable Castings Company, 1920. The foundry produced pipe fittings and sprinkler heads. The company is now owned by the ANVIL Corporation. LCHS D-10-03-43

Nickel deposits in Bart Township were discovered in the early 1700s, and attempts to mine them began soon thereafter. It wasn't until the Gap Mining Company was formed in 1849 that it became a real business. These employees, pictured circa 1890, worked around the mines extracting and smelting the ore. Identified at top left is Sam Armer. LCHS 2-08-03-18

Employees at the Posey Iron Works pause for a photo by machinery possibly used for galvanizing, circa 1940. Posey Iron Works evolved from the Lancaster Iron Works, a foundry and machine works that began in the 1830s. The original foundry was located at the southwest corner of Marion and Arch Streets. LCHS 2-02-02-73

Men pour molten iron into molds at the Posey Iron Works, circa 1950. LCHS 2-10-03-51

A Worldwide Giant Based in Lancaster

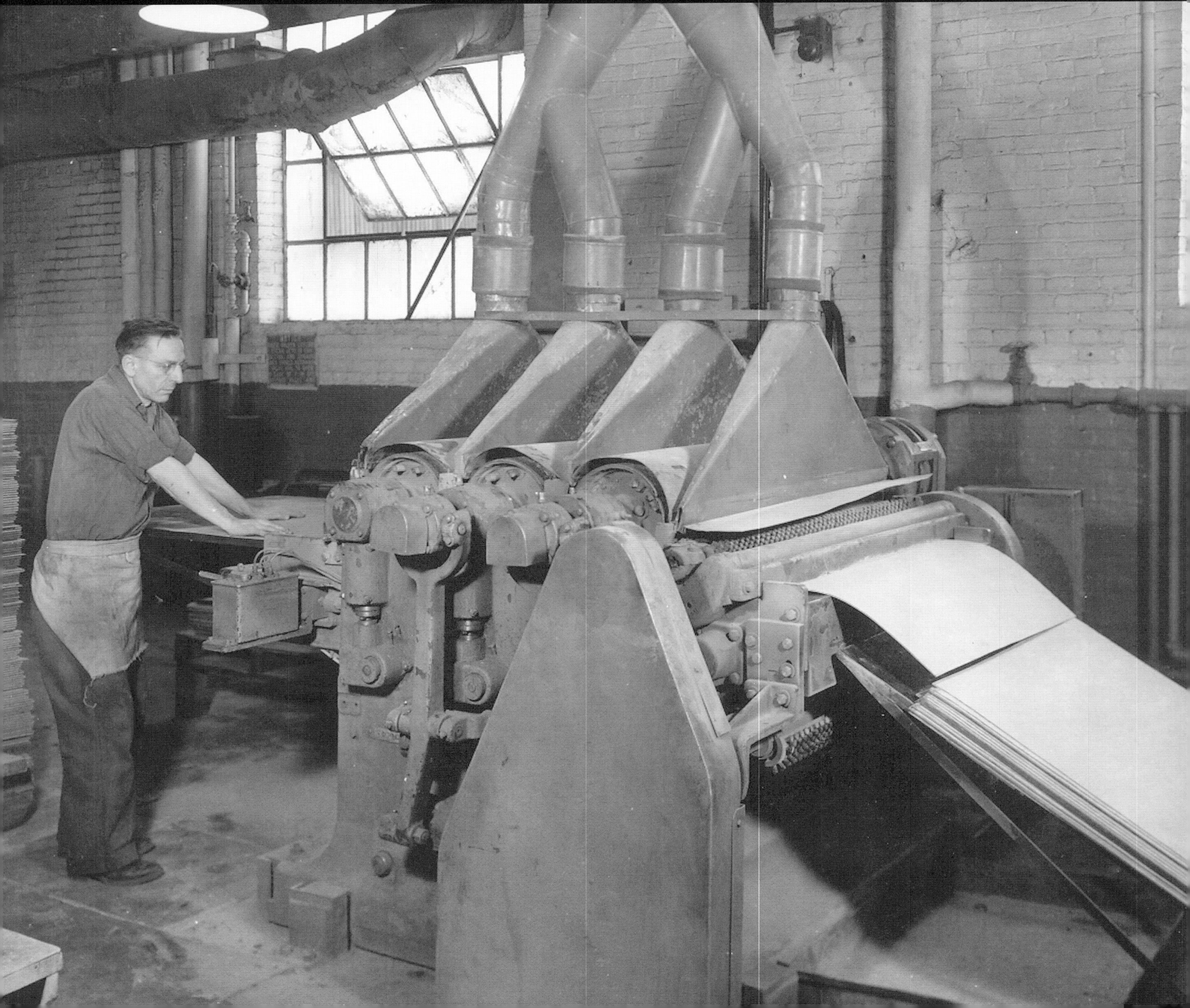

John Ward Willson Loose

Thomas Armstrong established his first cork works in Pittsburgh in 1860. By the mid-1890s, it had grown to be the largest such venture in the world and had taken over two local businesses: the Conestoga Cork Works, established by Harris Boardman, and Byron Dodge's Lancaster Cork Works.

With demand for cork decreasing, the company adapted by developing new uses for cork, such as corkboard. In 1907, Armstrong built a new plant on a cornfield in Manheim Township and in 1909 began rolling out sheets of linoleum flooring. The company also manufactured cork-backed flooring, bakelite closures, felt and insulation materials, and other cork products. The floor plant grew in size until it became Lancaster's biggest industry. By 1918, the plant employed 772 people and paid a minimum wage of 26 cents per hour.

During World War I, parts of Armstrong's facilities were adapted to make artillery shells for the government. When World War II began, the company obtained numerous government contracts for making armor-piercing shells, Navy Corsair fighter plane fuselages, camouflage netting, cartridge racks, and other materials. The workers' exceptional efforts earned the company the Army-Navy "E" Award, an honor won by just five percent of the businesses involved in wartime production.

continued...

Above: Production line workers check inlaid linoleum prior to pressing the ingredients (mainly ground cork, oxidized linseed oil, and color pigments), circa 1930. Armstrong Cork Company manufactured several kinds of linoleum, including Battleship, Jaspe, and inlaid. LCHS A-08-02-79

Left: Manufacturing Linotile at Armstrong, May, 1945. Sheets of Linotile were sanded for accurate thickness and then cut into tiles. LCHS 2-10-02-33

By mid-century, the company seemed like its own community. It had its own athletic association and a grocery store for employees on company grounds. Armstrong continued to develop new products built upon its traditional strengths: flooring, ceilings, cabinets. In the process the company pioneered the use of market research to guide the development of new consumer goods. Its potential liability for asbestos-related lawsuits, however, forced the company to file for reorganization under Chapter 11 bankruptcy laws in 2000. In October, 2006, Armstrong announced its emergence from bankruptcy.

Today, Armstrong World Industries operates forty-one plants in twelve different countries. Its headquarters remains in Lancaster, Pennsylvania.

Above: Benjamin H. Warfel, seated, inspects the floor covering prior to being trimmed into Quaker brand rugs or sheet flooring, circa 1925. Armstrong also produced flooring painted on felt-based backing. LCHS A-08-01-61

Right: The machine shop at the Armstrong Floor Plant is seen here in June of 1943. The American flag hanging from the ceiling helped boost morale during the height of Armstrong's war production efforts. LCHS 2-10-02-35

During World War II, the Armstrong Floor Plant fulfilled many government contracts for war materials. In this photo, circa 1944, the Floor Plant's final assembly line produces the front sections of fuselages for Corsair fighter planes. Armstrong's employees earned the company many excellence and efficiency awards, including the Army-Navy "E" Award. LCHS 2-06-05-02

Women box asphalt primer in the Lacquer Department at Armstrong in March, 1944. LCHS 2-10-02-39

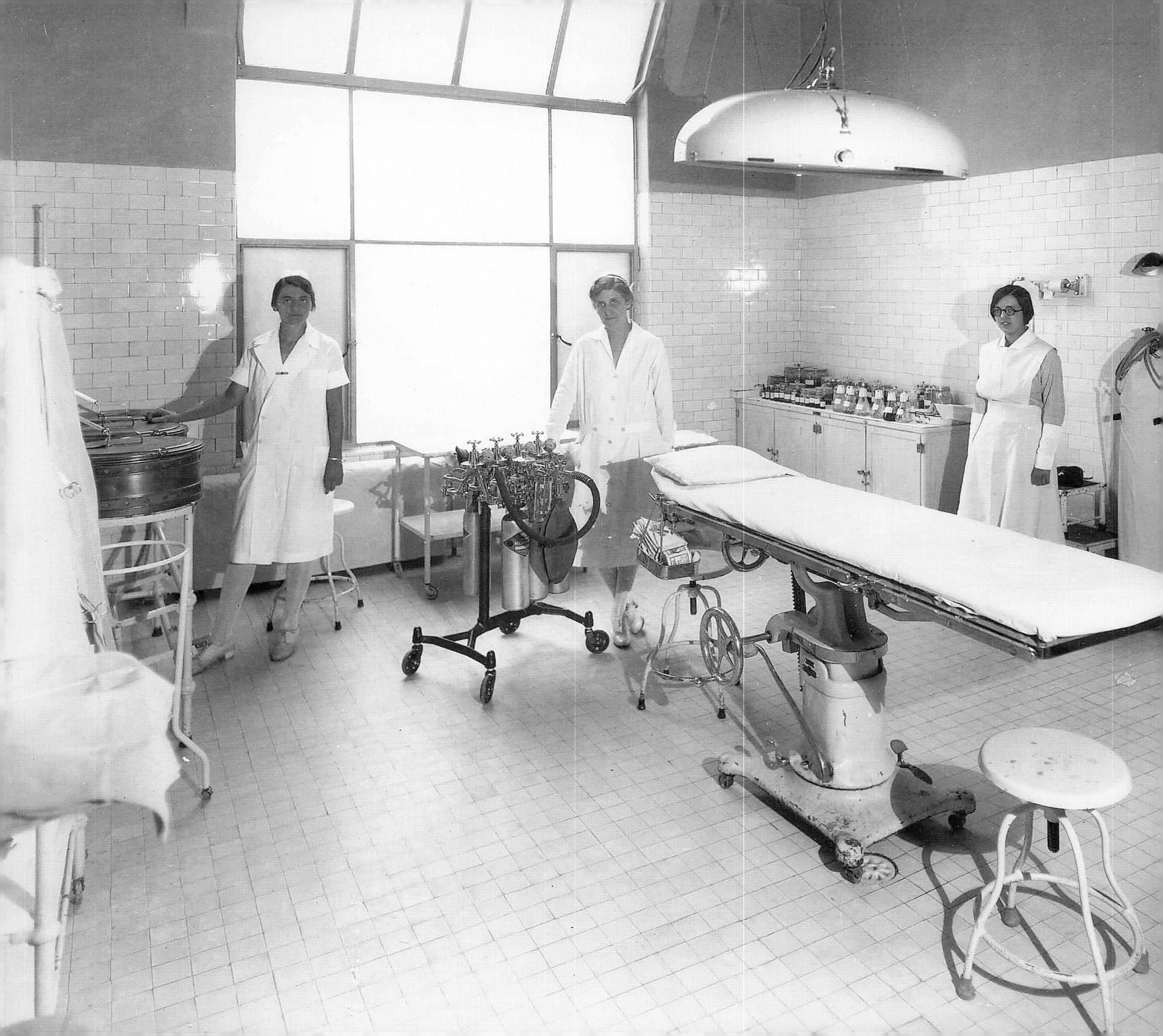

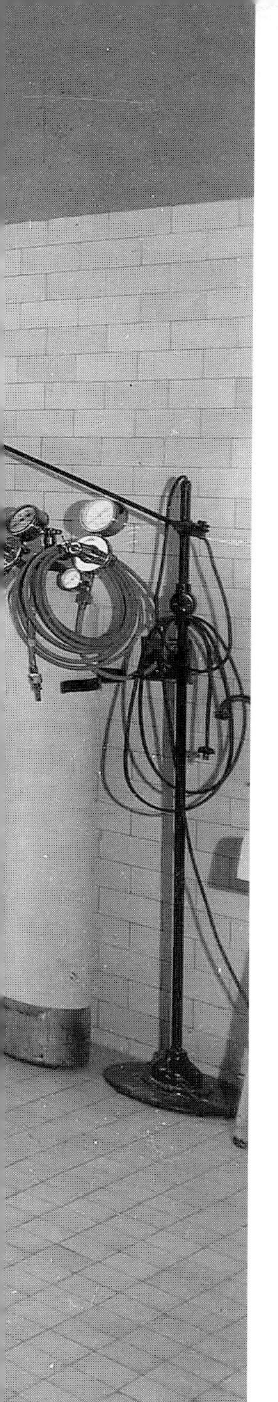

First Responders

John Ward Willson Loose

Public safety and care for the health of all persons serve as strong indicators of a community's response to its social obligations. Whether saving lives and property from fires or enforcing laws that govern society, Lancastrians have responded for nearly 250 years, much of that time voluntarily.

County records suggest that, as early as 1742, a fire company was active in what was then the borough of Lancaster. The Union Fire Company was more formally established in 1760, making it one of the nation's oldest volunteer fire companies. Seven active volunteer companies eventually provided fire protection for the community. In 1882 Lancaster City replaced them with a paid, professional fire department, only the third of its kind in the state of Pennsylvania.

Constables, sheriffs, and town police have long kept the peace. Mayor George Sanderson created Lancaster's police department in 1865. The force didn't have its own building until 1874. Subsequent police headquarters opened

continued…

Above: Lancaster Mayor George Sanderson, wearing a top hat, poses with his newly created police force in 1865. LCHS A-08-02-28

Left: By 1930, Lancaster General Hospital offered state-of-the-art surgical procedures in its operating rooms. LCHS D-02-02-17

in 1955 and 2004. County sheriffs, township, and borough police officers have kept the county safe for many years, as well.

Physicians, nurses, and midwives have cared for the health of Lancaster County residents since its inception. Military hospitals were set up at the Brothers' House of the Lititz Moravian Church and the Ephrata Cloister during the Revolutionary War. In 1797, the county established the office of the Directors of the Poor to look after the neediest citizens. The House of Employment, also known as the Almshouse, was built three years later, and in 1806 a separate hospital building was erected.

The city and county's growing health care needs required more hospitals, a demand met by St. Joseph's in 1883 (now Lancaster Regional Medical Center) and Lancaster General Hospital in 1893. Ephrata Community Hospital began operation in the 1920s, and more recently, the Heart of Lancaster Regional Medical Center opened in Lititz to serve the residents of northeastern Lancaster County.

Together the police, fire, and health care organizations of Lancaster County have established a long tradition of service to the community.

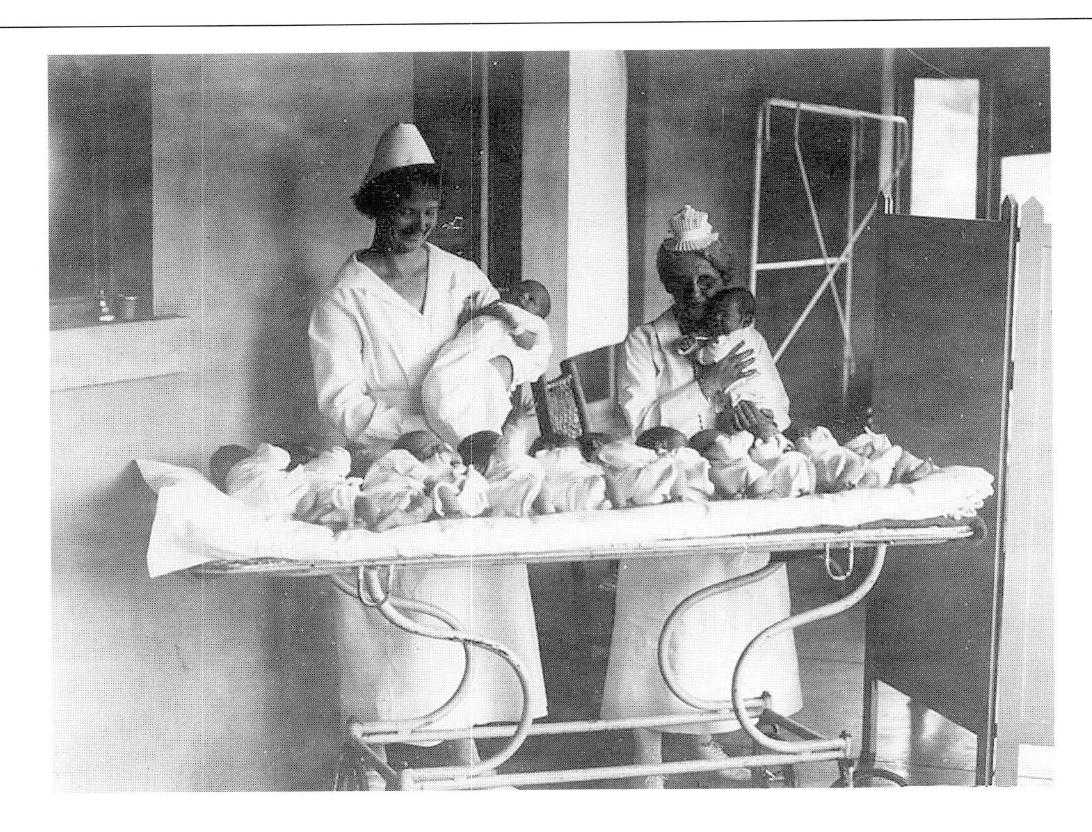

The nurses at St. Joseph's Hospital provided loving care to the newborn babies in the maternity ward. The Sisters of St. Francis of Philadelphia founded the hospital, located on Lancaster's College Avenue, in 1883. St. Joe's continues to provide health care to the county today as Lancaster Regional Medical Center. LCHS A-10-01-86

Nurses gather around one of St. Joseph's Hospital's first automobile ambulances, circa 1927. The hospital's Ladies Auxiliary donated the first one in 1916. LCHS A-10-02-61

A steam fire engine battles the famous blaze at Reilly Bros. & Raub hardware store on North Queen Street. The February 10, 1910, fire destroyed the store, which was located at 40–42 North Queen Street. LCHS 1-01-01-78

The men of Engine Company No. 4 pose with their horse-drawn ladder truck and steam engine outside of their firehouse at 333 North Queen Street in Lancaster, circa 1916. LCHS A-09-02-39

The men of Engine Company No. 1 show off their 1918 American LaFrance city service truck in front of the firehouse on West King Street in Lancaster in 1918. Standing from left are Captain Thomas Sperling, John Stout, Michael Andes, Harry Swope, and Harry Kurl. Frank Koerkle sits at the wheel. Lancaster put its first motorized fire apparatus into service in 1915. LCHS 2-02-02-57

The Lancaster Police Department sat for this photograph in 1894. Henry Hartley was chief of police at the time. LCHS A-08-02-31

The Lancaster City Police pause for a portrait in 1925. Seated in the front row from left to right are Detective Howard Anderson, Chief Guy Eckman, Mayor Frank Musser, Agnes Ferriter, and Detective George Parmer. Ms. Ferriter was Lancaster's first policewoman. Other notables included in this photo are Edward Millen (fourth row, center), Lancaster's first African-American police officer, and Sgt. Elwood Gainor (seated in the sidecar at left), who was shot in the line of duty two years later. His murder remains unsolved. LCHS A-10-01-51

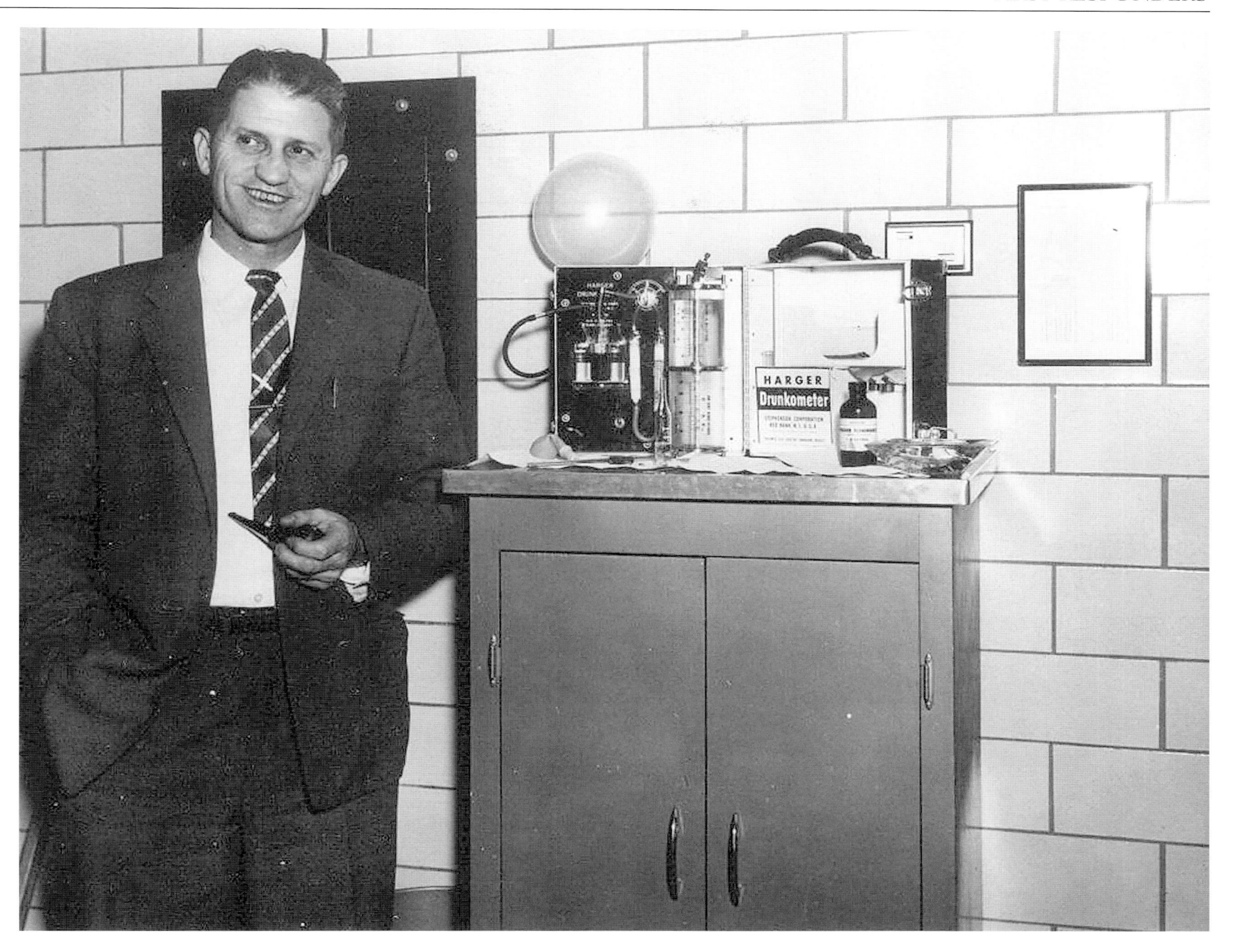

Lancaster Police Chief William Hershner introduces Pennsylvania's first Drunkometer, circa 1960. Similar to today's Breathalyzer™, the machine measured the amount of alcohol in a person's system. LCHS A-08-01-57

Driver Teddy Powell and Dr. Kelty prepare to pick up a patient in a Lancaster General Hospital horse-drawn ambulance, circa 1907. LCHS A-10-02-69

Marianne Heckles

In 1893, a group of concerned citizens, led by Reverend D. Wesley Bicksler of Salem Evangelical Church, decided to open a new hospital in the city of Lancaster. The group sought to provide more health care to the rapidly growing city, as its existing hospitals were often filled to capacity and unable to tend to everyone in need. By December, 1893, Lancaster General Hospital was established at 322 North Queen Street.

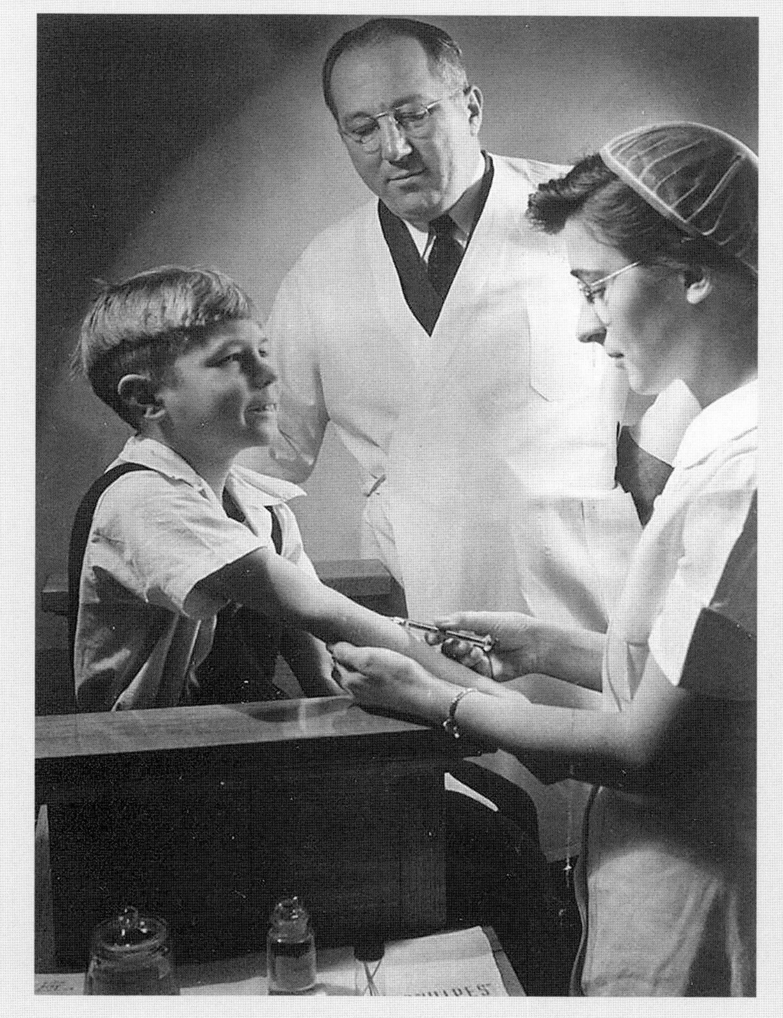

This first incarnation of Lancaster General had seven rooms and one ward for patients, as well as a reception room and superintendent's quarters. By 1896, the hospital had outgrown this site and moved its patients to the former Ezra F. Landis mansion at 530–532 North Lime Street. This location not only accommodated more patients, it was also more convenient to the railroad station and included an ambulance entrance on North Cherry Street.

Within its first twenty years, Lancaster General built three new wings (including a women's wing), acquired X-ray equipment, and opened a nursing school. In 1952 the hospital's capacity reached 450 beds, and by the 1960s it had become a true urban hospital, capable of treating all of Lancaster's health care needs. It became the county's first hospital to have a fully accredited trauma center in 1987.

In more recent years, Lancaster General has branched out across the county. The Lancaster General Health Campus opened in 1994 to offer a convenient central location for lab tests and doctor visits, and in 2000 Lancaster General gave birth to its Women and Babies Hospital, dedicated to the health-care needs of women. With these facilities and outpatient centers from Elizabethtown to Willow Street, Lancaster General Hospital grew to become the county's largest employer. Today's health-care professionals continue the hospital's long history of providing high-quality medical services to the community.

Above: A young boy sits bravely as Nurse Landis administers his polio vaccination with Dr. Steven Lockey Sr. looking on. LCHS A-08-01-86

Above: Clean linens were a must in the laundry department of the Lancaster General Hospital. These ladies kept them spotless, circa 1930. LCHS D-02-02-15

Right: Nurses go over their notes at a nurses' station at Lancaster General, circa 1930. LCHS D-02-02-16

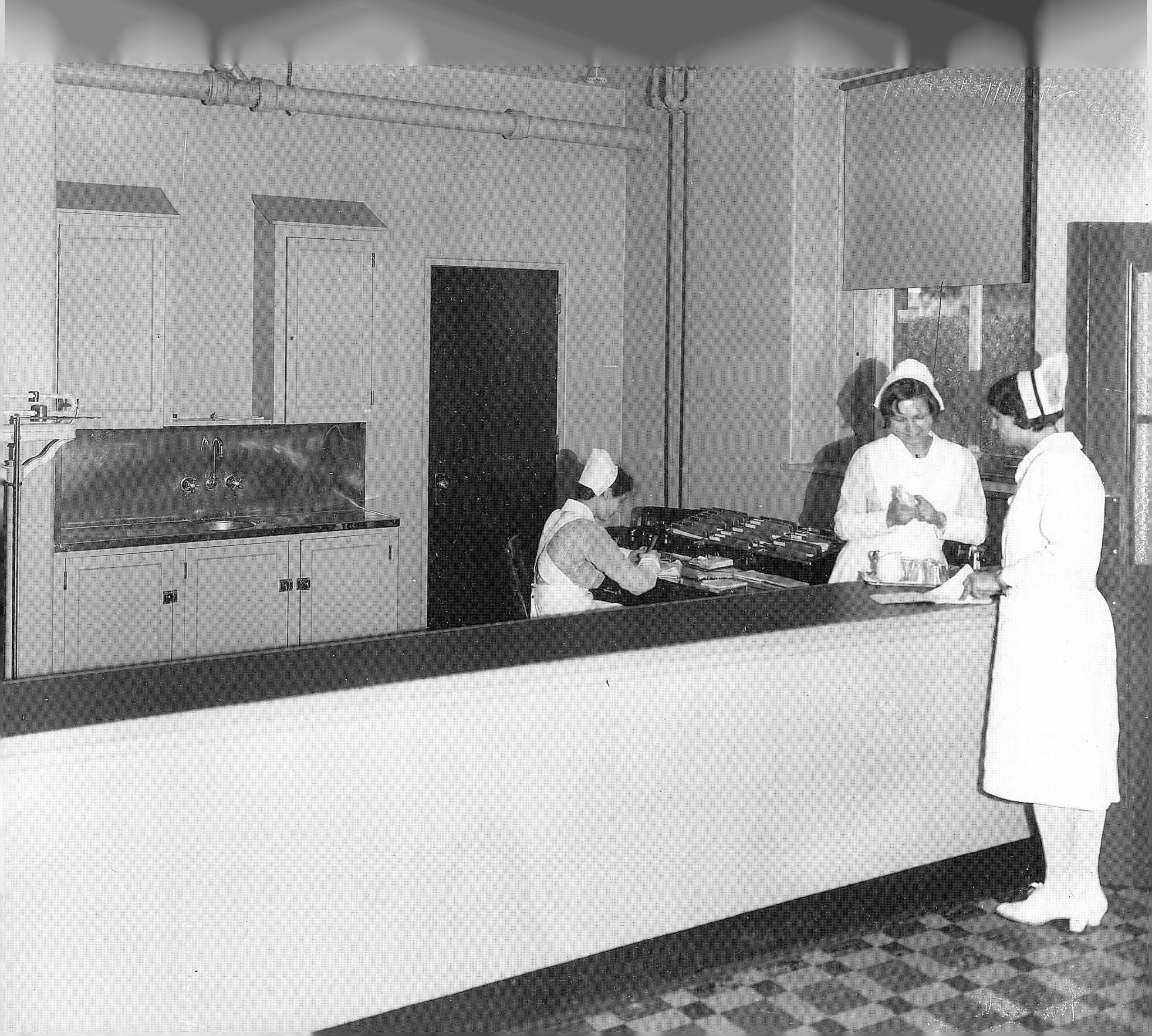

Contributors

LINDA S. ALECI, Ph.D., is an associate professor of art history at Franklin & Marshall College, having earned her doctorate from Princeton University. She curated the Lancaster County Historical Society's 2005 exhibition *MarketPlace: Lancaster Central Market and the Making of Community*.

MARIANNE HECKLES is a graduate of Kutztown University. She is a research assistant and coordinator of photograph collections of the Lancaster County Historical Society.

WILLIAM E. KRANTZ is a retired Lancaster businessman and a graduate of Franklin & Marshall College. He is a member of the Publications Committee of the Lancaster County Historical Society.

GERALD S. LESTZ spent nearly forty years as a staff writer and editor for the *Lancaster New Era* and launched "The Scribbler" column, which continues to this day. He has written nearly a dozen books on Lancaster history and the Amish and was the prime mover in establishing Lancaster's historic districts. He is a Fellow of the Lancaster County Historical Society.

JOHN WARD WILLSON LOOSE is editor-in-chief of the *Journal of the Lancaster County Historical Society* as well as a Fellow of the Lancaster County Historical Society (FLCHS). He graduated from Millersville State Teachers College, now Millersville University, and taught for many years in the Donegal School District

BARRY R. RAUHAUSER is the Stauffer Curator at the Lancaster County Historical Society. He graduated with a B.A. from Penn State University and an M.A. from the University of Delaware's Winterthur Program in Early American Culture.

continued…

THOMAS R. RYAN, Ph.D., is the executive director of the Lancaster County Historical Society. He has a master's degree from the Winterthur Program in Early American Culture as well as a doctorate in American Civilization from the University of Delaware. He has taught at Franklin & Marshall College and Millersville University.

HEATHER S. TENNIES is the archivist at the Lancaster County Historical Society. She holds a master's degree in library science from the University of Kentucky.

Index

(* indicates photograph)